ON THE
WAY OF FREEDOM

by

Roel Kaptein

with the co-operation of

Duncan Morrow

THE COLUMBA PRESS
1993

First edition, 1993, published by
THE COLUMBA PRESS
93 The Rise, Mount Merrion, Blackrock, Co Dublin, Ireland

Cover by Bill Bolger
Diagrams by Duncan Morrow
Origination by The Columba Press
Printed by Loader Jackson Printers, Arlesey

ISBN 1 85607 0778

For Frank Wright
an unforgettable friend
1948—1993

Contents

'Think of the lilies growing in the fields; they never have to work or spin; yet I assure you that not even Solomon in all his regalia was robed like one of these. Now if that is how God clothes the grass in the field which is there today and thrown into the furnace tomorrow, will he not look after you much more, you men of little faith.' – *Matthew 6:28-30*

Preface

During the 1980s and 90s, we, members of the Corrymeela Community, have been working together exploring the gospel, the bible and our lives, trying to find ways forward for our thinking, for our actions and for our lives. In the course of these experiences together, we have had many insights. We have tried to draw models of what we saw, trying to make clearer what we already saw with our eyes, 'the eyes of our being'. We have gathered together some of our discoveries, in the hope that they can become something like an ancient 'enchiridion' for those who read it: a book that we carry in our hands, in our minds and in our hearts. We hope that it is a book which helps each of us to find and stay on the path, not straying off into the realms of 'common sense and the anxieties of this world.'

Introduction

René Girard

The book you are about to read is full of penetrating insight about the strange ways of human desire and the conflicts it generates, not only among nations but among neighbours, and inside ourselves as well.

Much of this insight relates to a central thesis about human desire which is most simply and directly formulated at the beginning. This thesis consists in denying that our desires are really our own. We borrow them from other people.

When we intensely desire someone or something, we feel that between us and whatever we desire, a unique affinity exists that is the cause of our desire. Not so, says Roel Kaptein. As a rule, our desires are prompted by a third person or by many persons who are really models we imitate. Whatever we desire seems desirable because of them.

This conception of desire is called mimetic or imitative desire. Very often this mimetic desire operates through desire itself. We desire an object, in other words, because someone else already desires it. When such is the case, mimetic desire generates two identical desires for the same object, two rival desires. As a result, the model and his imitator become obstacles in each other's path. This is called mimetic rivalry.

Mimetic rivalry is perfectly normal, natural and we do not have to feel guilty about it. We must realise, however, that it can easily lead us into temptation. The mutual interference between model and imitator is likely to inflame the two desires more and more. And this escalation of desire, in turn, quickly leads to the type of conflict that is most widespread among human beings, the type of reciprocal violence for which each side always blames the other, the violence that has plagued mankind since the beginning of history.

The more conflictual our imitation of desire becomes, the more we resent our dependence upon our rival, the less willing we are to acknowledge the truth which we try to hide even and especially from ourselves. This dissimulation is usually quite successful in the sense that the suppressed desire becomes completely invisible and that even the psychopathological symptoms that it may generate seem unrelated to it.

Since the beginning of the modern age, philosophers and scientists have deprived human beings of many treasured beliefs, now discarded as superstition. Mankind has been stripped bare of all the comforting myths that had flourished undisturbed for thousands of years, the conviction of each culture, for instance, that it is the navel of the universe.

No one had really tried, until now, to take away our desire; no one had yet claimed that our desire is not really ours. Intense desire is not particularly enjoyable; it is often quite painful. We used to comfort ourselves with the thought that it is rooted very deep inside of us, that it expresses our 'authentic self', 'our true personality'. This was our last egotistical satisfaction and mimetic desire deprives us of it.

Freud made a first move in that direction, of course, He included other people beside ourselves in the genesis of our desires, but only very special people and very few, the two who play the most important role in our upbringing. Freud, besides, took the precaution of presenting this parental involvement in such a way as not to offend our feeling of uniqueness, as desiring creatures.

Freud allowed only two persons in our inner sanctum, Roel Kaptein lets in a whole crowd. We are reminded of the Gospel's story in which a man seemed possessed by a single demon and then thousands were expelled from his body, an entire Legion.

When they first become acquainted with mimetic desire, some people feel as if they had been unexpectedly submerged in water very cold and very deep. Instead of scrambling out as fast as they can, they should try swimming. After a few strokes, they will feel invigorated. They will discover that Roel unravels many situations and attitudes that made no sense before; their respect for his method will increase.

After they finish this book, the readers will be grateful to the author. My own feeling is one of gratitude as well, for all the reasons that the readers will share with me, and also for more personal reasons. For many years, Roel and I have been studying mimetic desire together. His ideas in this book are also my ideas but he brings something to them that makes them more vivid once again.

My confidence in these ideas has never wavered but the youthful vigor of Roel's book has renewed my enthusiasm and, mimetically no doubt, I feel more creative once again. For this too I must be grateful.

This rejuvenation is not due solely to the style and even to the content of this book. More important than both is the spirit which created it. When we analyze mimetic entanglements merely for the sake of demonstrating that we ourselves are never fooled by the apparent spontaneity of desire, the whole exercise becomes futile, even a little sinister. Imitative desire wants nothing more than to be free from imitation. Complete self-sufficiency is its ultimate idol. If it were the author's goal as well, he would move away from genuine spontaneity which is not the absence of mimetic behaviour but the most naïve and innocent imitation of all, that of a little child, the attitude recommended by Jesus.

This book is luminous because the author never tries to demonstrate his cleverness at the reader's expense. He achieves real balance between the heart and the mind, easily avoiding the twin pitfalls of our time, an exclusive reliance on dry-as-dust pseudo-science on the one hand, and the mindless embrace of sentimental exhortation on the other, the pious anti-intellectualism that is a hidden form of nihilism. Our intellect demands to be fed along with our souls. And there is nothing wrong with trying to solve the puzzle of human self-deception, as long as our enterprise is neither manipulative nor prompted by a spirit of resentment against our fellow men.

Dostoevsky wrote somewhere that science will never manage to imprison mankind in a series of scientific principles and formulae. As soon as science claims that it has succeeded, dissenters will appear who will do whatever has to be done to prove the scientists wrong. They will act and think in such ways as to transgress the limitations that have been assigned to the human condition.

Like many ideas of Dostoevsky, this one seems prophetic of our time. more particularly of the situation in the social and psychological sciences. On the one hand, we still have the painstaking positivists and cognitivists doggedly trying to imprison all human behaviour in some rigid network of mathematical measurements; on the other hand, we have swarms of sceptics and nihilists who think and act in such ways that their purpose must be the one defined by the Russian novelist. They must be trying to demonstrate that a scientific definition of man is impossible.

Dostoevsky is proved right. But the question of what, actually, is being proved remains unclear. Does the present situation demonstrate that there can be no such thing as a valid knowledge of man?

If by knowledge we mean the complete inventory that the old positivism was dreaming about, the type of knowledge that would make all future behaviour predictable, turning 'human engineering' into a 'real science', the answer is no. The nihilists are right to deny that this type of knowledge can be achieved.

Does it follow, then, that science should confess its own bankruptcy and bow to the superior wisdom of modern nihilism? I do not think so. Mimetic rivalry easily accounts for the rival stubborness of what is really academic infighting. The nihilists desire the same thing as the scientists and, one against the other, the two schools of thought can play what Roel calls 'the game of culture', mimetic competition. The nihilists too are looking for absolute knowledge, but of a negative sort, the absolute certainty that no certainty can be achieved. The goal is the same on both sides. Against the increasingly sterile certainties of scientistic research, the nihilists uphold the even more sterile certainties of their nihilism. This is a nice example of mimetic rivalry.

Should we claim, then, that the mimetic theory constitutes the 'hard' knowledge for which science has been looking? If we did, we would be playing the 'game of culture' ourselves, a game that Roel wisely refuses to play. In the expression 'hard knowledge', the first word is highly significant. A knowledge is 'hard' if, instead of breaking apart when hit, it hits back and destroys its would-be destroyers.

Is not the search for 'hard' knowledge really a search for a weapon so powerful that it will force itself upon the unbelievers? Roel never tries to give his theorising this kind of hardness. To him, it is an act of love and edification, not of petty demystification and deconstruction.

The real Christian spirit is not a mediocre compromise between a reason and a faith forever destined to be each other's enemies, a timid avoidance of investigative freedom, but the very reverse, an all-out effort towards the unknown, sustained by the hope that, in the end, reason and faith must come together once again and, like two long lost friends, they will joyously embrace. This is the hope that made this book possible.

As we read it, our pleasure is compounded by the thought that, unlike machines, books never break down and this one will always be with us, ready at hand whenever we feel like renewing acquaintance with it, just for the fun of it perhaps, or with some more specific purpose in mind, because of some difficult situation in our lives, perhaps, one that requires special guidance. This book does not resemble those fair weather friends that make themselves scarce in times of hardship; it is one of the trusted few that are always around when needed, ready to give sound advice when sound advice is sought.

Entrance : The face of the victim

Our culture* increasingly gives us the impression that we are atomised individuals, responsible for and to ourselves and free to do what we want. Inevitably in this situation, everybody and everything else become tools which we can use to reach our own goals. Others get in the way between us and our goals.

When we see other people scapegoating* and blaming others, we despise it. However, in despising and loathing it we actually prove that we are not free of it ourselves. Instead we show that we know all about it. Nevertheless, we continue to scapegoat* and blame others, over and over again, without ever acknowledging what we are doing. Even while we are doing it, we remain absolutely certain that we ourselves are not scapegoating*. We are sure that we are simply right!

Given this situation, everything which is in this enchiridion, indeed even everything which we learn from the gospel can be used to play the game of scapegoating*, the game of culture*, better. We can become even cleverer hypocrites, thinking ourselves superior. There is only one possibility of escape from this cycle; to recognise the scapegoat* mechanism operating through us. We know that time and again we are made scapegoats* ourselves. We fight to escape this predicament by scapegoating* others. The alternative, a wholly different possibility, is to find the freedom* to let it be. We can stop the fighting and so be free at last.

How do we go about this? How can we find a way to this possibility? Emmanuel Levinas, the great Jewish thinker, talks of the defenceless face of the other which shows itself to us in a way we can't avoid. When we recognise this face, it makes us a captive. This face is the face of the scapegoat*, the victim, helpless and without possibility of escape. When we see this face, it shows us ourselves and our helplessness. We can only bow and serve.

In this way, the gospels ask us to look at Jesus, who shows us who we are, bringing us to the place we must find in order to find new life, freedom. It is the place we fear most, that of the scapegoat*.

We can only read the following text in a constant to and fro between this truth and the text itself. Otherwise we will be more enclosed in culture*, instead of finding a way out of it.

PART ONE

Culture: Our World

This is a short description of our world, the world in which we live and strive. This is the world which keeps us alive. At the same time we want to change this world for a new world. This change will only be possible if we ourselves change. Indeed, it will only be possible if we become open to the possibility of being changed.

It may be that we can really change only if we first accept who we are as members of the culture* in which we find ourselves. At the same time, we assume, although it does not actually matter whether it is true or not, that we can only know about our human situation when we are also aware of another possibility, aware of the new world. In learning about what it means to be new people, we also learn about the old, about who we are now.

* Words marked* are defined in a glossary on page 136.

1. Human life and human relationships

In the modern age, our culture*, everything which teaches us about who we are, gives us the impression that we are separate and complete individuals. The best symbol for our age is the motor car. Each car is complete with its own boundaries and shape. The impact of the person in one car on the being of a person in another is limited. Within this form, each of us has a separate existence.

Of course, there may be times when we want to signal to others about our intentions. Nevertheless, the degree of communication is limited and nothing essential happens except aging. Each 'individual' is a clearly limited and formed being.

This view of people as separate and complete individuals has huge consequences for our lives. One of these is the desire of every person to know their 'rights' and to fight for them against intruders. A second consequence is that freedom* is seen as the freedom* to escape every restriction. We all long for the freedom* to do what we want, when we want, as we want. Of course, we are constantly brought up against the reality that this is not possible, and despite this each of us strives to achieve the maximum number of possibilities. Freedom* is a commodity like any other. Each of us must strive to be the richest, the most powerful, the most beautiful, the cleverest, the fastest and so on. In order to achieve our goals we are tempted to, or actually do, break every rule. The fact that everybody and everything in life is being used by us as a tool to reach our own goals becomes truer all the time.

In fact this individualism is an illusion. We are not autonomous and separated, nor are we complete and unchanging. Each of us is born in a specific place, at a specific time. In the same way each of us is born into particular relationships. In the first instance, our closest relationship is to our mother, who in turn is a person who carries her own history and who in and has lived in many different relationships throughout her life. Through her we come into relationship with the world, both past and present. After birth, we come into relationships with other people, who each have their own relationships. Our whole life is lived in many different relationships, each with their own importance at different times in our life and all of them constantly changing.

Most of the time we are not aware of the importance of particular relationships in our lives. Mostly we do not know the influences which are shaping our actions, judgements and lives at a given moment. In our relationships we change and move, learning and following, imitating and reflecting, nearly always without consciously knowing it. We are and 'become' in our relationships to others, changing in different ways all the time.

Change is not only a matter of consciousness. Change happens in our lives at every level, both conscious and unconscious. Most of the change in our lives happens without our control or assent and without our knowing it. In fact, the origin of all change is a much deeper reality than consciousness, which we call mimesis*.

All relationships are characterised by mimesis*. Mimesis* was originally a Greek word meaning to imitate or mimic. However, in everyday speech imitation and mimicry are conscious experiences. We use the Greek word to emphasise that change in human relationships is not primarily a matter of conscious imitation. Mimesis* is between us, irrespective of whether we know it and wish it or not.

Each of us is born into, and lives in, our own particular and unique relationships. Each of us is always different from everybody else, a unique person. We do not need to worry about this. Each of us is unique and, at the same time, we always belong to everybody and everything around us, always being a part of the whole.

The fact that our personal uniqueness is only possible because we live together with so many other people turns the world of individualism upside down. This means that the nature of our relationships, the question of with whom or what we are in mimesis*, is very important.

Another consequence is that we can never be really in control of our lives. By far the greatest part of our lives is given to us by others. We cannot live without others, because they are our very life.

Furthermore, the endless struggling to win in the race of modern life results in the sacrifice of all relationships, and so of the reality of our lives, for an illusory goal, which we call freedom* . In fact it is the goal of winning over everybody else – the goal of control. Freedom*, in the modern sense, proves to be slavery because even if we reach our goal to be the most important person or to have the most important object or characteristic we are doomed to have to defend it against our imitators and rivals for ever. In the end we always lose, ultimately when we lose our rivalry against death. In fact, freedom* in our modern culture* is the feeling of winning in the struggles of our relationships and it always brings with it the anxiety that we may lose tomorrow.

The idea that we are formed, original, autonomous persons is a serious misunderstanding. As long as we believe ourselves to be 'formed' or 'original' we are probably making it very difficult for ourselves to change. As a result we are and remain who we are, as we are. We are even proud of the fact. Because it is unchanging, our being becomes our predicament, our permanent prison.

The central importance of our relationships turns upside down our modern ideas of independence and autonomy. Our relationships with others are the source and reality of our own being. Relationships are not within our control, they are given to us. In turn we give to others. How we 'are' crucially depends on the relationships we live in and their content. The big question for each of us is how do we find real freedom*, the world and our lives being as they are?

2. Mimesis

All of us are in relationships both past and present. Therefore we are always in mimesis*. Mimesis is always going on between us. I do what you do because you are doing it. You do what I do because I do it, and so on. In every human culture* all mimesis* is the mimesis* of desire. We take on and react to each others' desires to have or to get something or somebody without even knowing it. I desire what you desire because you desire it. The object of our desire can be anything: a man, a woman, a reputation, a car, a position, a house, a job and so on. Getting our desires from one another is mimesis*. Between human beings is always the mimesis* of desire. No human life is separate from the lives of others.

Of course, if we all desire the same thing, the result can only be a clash – violence. The great enigma of human experience and reality is that human life comes from, consists of, and at the same time is destroyed by mimesis*. The Genesis story of Adam and Eve in Eden is an attempt to explain this .

I desire what you desire because you desire it and you desire it more because I desire it. This desire is always the desire to have, to appropriate, to get. Desire is mimetic.

We usually assume that our desires arise spontaneously within us. In other words, we desire somebody or something 'simply' because we like them or it. It 'just happens'. We assume that the desire has no history outside of ourselves. In fact, every time we use words like 'simply' or 'just' we should be very suspicious. We are often hiding something, often something very important. In the case of our desires, we are wrong to think that they arise 'simply because we like something.'

Desire is never a simple relationship between the desiring person and the desired object. Our desire always involves somebody else. Our desire is always triangular, involving three not two points; the other who is already desiring, ourselves and the desired person or object. The other in each case is an important person for us, for whatever reason. For example, the other might be our father or mother, they might look like one of them or they might be somebody we regard as successful. In fact they could be anybody. The other is always somebody whom we envy. In a diagram it would look like this:

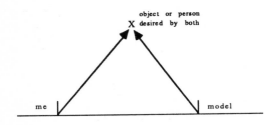

From the diagram, we can see that we are both desiring the same object and automatically we have become each other's rivals. We fight with each other, escalating the fight, building up against each other.

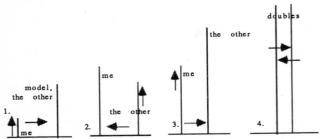

In the course of the fight the other – our rival – becomes more and more important. We forget about the original issue of the conflict, the original object of desire. In fact it eventually disappears. The fight becomes only a matter of power between the two rivals. In fighting, everything outside the fight becomes less and less important. Our world shrinks and we become more and more like one another. Eventually we become doubles, exactly the same. Ultimately, everything ends up in chaos[3].

Increasingly, this situation is the reality of modern life, for people in their private lives, for groups and for nations. Life, for each person, for nations and for the world is permanently in turmoil, close to possible or actual violence.

There are so many examples. In relationships, two men fight one another over a woman until they become absolutely fascinated with one another, doubles. In companies, employees rival with one another for the attention of the boss. Unless the rivalry ends, they may end up sacrificing their career in order to destroy their rival. In Northern Ireland, two groups rival with one another, both sure that they are completely different from one another and yet, for people outside, they become evermore similar. Ultimately the fight is about nothing, with the permanent threat that the whole place could end up in absolute chaos, as actually happened at times in the Lebanon or Yugoslavia. All of us are in model-rival* relationships and as a result we become more and more identical. For forty years the Cold War threatened to destroy all differences between the West and the East, with the potential that it could end in the absolute destruction of both groups.

As we become more identical, we rival with one another more easily. This in itself provokes further chaos. Because we are alike, we all desire to be the only person with this or that quality, to have specific 'objects' or 'qualities'. In fact we are all striving to be different. But because we are all fighting in mimesis* with one another, we end up with what we want to avoid. The fight to be different means more rivalry. In our fighting we become more and more alike.

There is another possible relationship arising from the mimesis* of desire. Instead of struggling rivals, we become absolute obstacles for one another. In the model-obstacle* relationship, I seek a model who is so great that I can never win. No matter how hard I rival with my model, I always lose. The attraction of this model is that were I to win, I would in a sense conquer the whole world. The very unreachable height of my model is what makes him or her attractive. If I could succeed in overcoming an obstacle of such enormity, then I could feel more or less like a god. However, the fact that I choose such a big obstacle means that I will always lose. As a result of my endless losing, I become depressed, and have the feeling that it is senseless.

Anybody or anything might become an obstacle for me. My model-obstacle* might be another person, whom I admire, or some kind of ideal. It might be a wish to be totally pure, to be like Christ, or the wish to be stronger than an enemy who is clearly stronger than I am. In fact, all striving which is doomed to failure brings us into the model-obstacle* relationship.

The objects of model-obstacle* relationship often appear to be very beautiful, very worthwhile, very lofty things. The desire to be like Christ might be an example. But because it is impossible it throws us deeper and deeper into a pit of depression. We become obsessed by our ideal, our goal and destroy ourselves in the process. In a model we can try to show this.

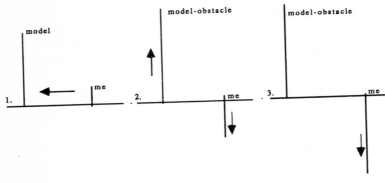

Very often we experience rivalry as simply (!) exciting or enjoyable. At first it involves playing, teasing, trying our hardest, trying to 'achieve'. But all the time there is the possibility that, unexpectedly, violence will erupt between the players, whether the players are two people in their personal lives or superpowers risking the whole world. Alternatively, because of the rivalry, we might be very depressed. Ultimately it can result in hysterical behaviour or schizophrenia.

The model-obstacle* relationship, like the model-rival* relationship, is very common in our culture*. There are numerous examples. A professor might become a model-obstacle* for his student. The student strives to become a more important scholar than his or her professor and makes the professor much more important than he is, because only a great model is worth striving to overcome. At the same time, the student becomes so paralysed that he can't pass his basic exams. He makes the professor an absolute obstacle for himself. It can also happen the other way round if a professor wants to be an extremely important man with many disciples and yet none of his students finish their doctorates. In fact, the professor makes himself an absolute obstacle for the students.

In the model-obstacle* relationship there is always fascination* with the model. This fascination* can be very beautiful. However, deep down, though it is often hidden, there is depression. In one way or another we know that the goal is unreachable, even though we don't want to know it and avoid admitting it.

On the other hand, model-obstacle* relationships sometimes lead to compulsive, obsessive behaviour. We continually make attempts to reach our goal even though we never get away from the start. Our attempts are characterised by a deep desperation. Deep down there is great violence in the rivalry with the obstacle which could erupt at any time, even killing the obstacle which we ourselves chose. This is the background to crimes of passion where the girl who did not desire the man is killed, or the man kills himself. Living in a model-obstacle* relationship (which comes to be the meaning of our whole life) is in a sense a form of slow death. Ultimately it might result in some kind of psychosis.[4]

3. Spatial and temporal mimesis

In some ways it is difficult to understand that we are always in mimesis*. We can see the situation a little more clearly if we differentiate between the mimesis* which is going on in all our relationships at the present moment, that is 'spatial mimesis*', and the mimesis* which goes on between our present self and our own past (and even the past of our ancestors) which we call temporal mimesis*.

When we are born we have no personal history. From the very beginning, or even from conception, we are in mimesis* with surrounding people, in the first instance with our mother. We are, so to speak, in one 'space' with our mother. Observing the mother with all of the means the child has, the child imitates or mimics her, learning everything. This is spatial mimesis*. At every point of our existence, each of us lives within a multitude of relations – with people, groups, nations, ideas, ideologies and so on. All of these make up the totality of the mimetic field in which each of us is living at a particular moment. Now, at this very moment, we are in mimesis* with everything in and around us. This is spatial mimesis*. Sociology is the science which tries to clarify what is happening between groups and people in spatial mimesis*.

Throughout our lives we are in spatial mimesis* with each other and with everything around us. Were we not in spatial mimesis*, we could not learn, we could not change. In every meeting, we come into mimesis* with those we meet. Jesus, coming into our lives, asks us to follow him. This is spatial mimesis*.[5]

We learn by repetition, by doing what we have done before. We do what we do now because we once learned it. We are now in mimesis* with ourselves in the past, in a mimesis* in time. This we call temporal mimesis*. Once we have learnt something, we repeat automatically, in mimesis* with ourselves, unless something happens in the present to change us. All of this happens to us without us doing any further conscious thinking or acknowledgement. Through repetition of things once learnt, through temporal mimesis*, we get our 'character' or 'personality'. Our personal history, through temporal mimesis*, influences our acting and being and shapes us now. The same is true for groups. We are here in the field of (social) psychology. It is temporal mimesis* which gives us continuity. Without temporal mimesis* there would not be human life.

Mimesis* with experiences in the past is a great human reality; it is also the great human problem. Among all of our learning, we also endlessly repeat all of the things which we have learnt wrongly. In doing this, we are imprisoned in our own temporal mimesis*. Temporal mimesis* is therefore also the background to all of our endlessly repeated mistakes, all of our neuroses and psychoses and all of our unfreedom. The only possibility of escaping this mimesis* – of escaping slavery and unfreedom – is to meet a person in the present , who lives in another world. In mimesis* with them we are changed. In other words, we change by crossing the lines of temporal mimesis* (what we learnt in the past) with new lines of spatial mimesis*, in mimesis* with something new in the present. We ourselves find freedom* by meeting others who free us from our own history and eventually our culture*. We can try to show temporal and spatial mimesis* in a model:

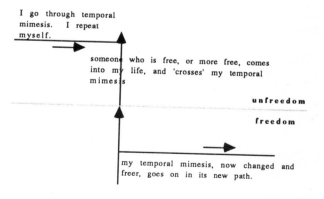

I go through temporal mimesis. I repeat myself.

someone who is free, or more free, comes into my life, and 'crosses' my temporal mimesis

unfreedom

freedom

my temporal mimesis, now changed and freer, goes on in its new path.

Of course reality is much more complicated than this diagram. In fact there are always countless influences on us from outside which change our temporal mimesis*, and which change us. Even more importantly, these changes are not always positive. In terms of our diagram, we can end up further away from freedom*. For example, an experience in the present of violence or rivalry can bring us into more unfreedom, which is the basis of further temporal mimesis*. Nevertheless, it remains true that decisive positive 'cuttings' or 'crossings' are possible.

Real change can happen in spatial mimesis* with another who is free, for example through a deep experience of being loved, experiences of friendship and even in the opportunities provided by psychotherapy and other related professions. In the gospel, when Jesus meets people, he cuts through their lines of temporal mimesis*. When he is in the same space as me, he changes me. He makes it impossible for me to stay the same and to go on repeating over and over again in temporal mimesis* with myself. People who meet him come into a spatial mimesis* with him and all of the old rivalry, learnt in temporal mimesis*, falls away. Meeting him, they are healed.

A beautiful example of this is given in John's Gospel in the story of the sick man at the healing pool of Bethesda. In the story, the man is said to have been lying sick at the pool for 38 years. He has never reached the pool at the crucial time when the angel of the Lord disturbed the waters. Others always beat him to it. He was always in rivalry, he always lost, and he remained sick. When he meets Jesus, the man is freed from the rivalry and he is cured.[6]

4. Plus and minus are the same

In a culture* there are structures*, ways of ordering things. Because there are structures, everybody has his or her own place. Because these places are fixed, everybody can compare his or her place with the place of others. Others are 'higher' and 'lower'– they are different. In a structured setting, relationships are clear.

In a world or culture* in which structure* has disappeared there are no fixed places. In the absence of structures, everybody can rival with everybody else. Nobody has a steady place, everybody's place is uncertain. Ultimately, only mimesis* remains. Everyone and everything goes up and down in accordance with the mimetic games and fights. In the end we can no longer really speak of 'up' and 'down'. Up and down only have meaning when there are fixed points from which we can measure them. Without structures, all of our comparisons are only valid for the moment we compare. Life therefore becomes a constant struggle with no possibility of winning.

Because there are no longer any fixed points, clear relationships with one another become impossible. Clear relationships are made impossible when we can no longer refer to anything which is objectively valid for us all. If that has disappeared, we are left with the constant shifts in mimetic rivalry between us. How we feel, how we are depends only on our position within the mimetic rivalries, on whether we are winning or losing.

We are always in model-rival* or model-obstacle* relationships. These relationships are always ambivalent and never clear. I may love my rival, seeing that he has things which I don't have. I admire him and nevertheless I fight against him in an attempt to get what he has, to win in the rivalry. At one and the same time, in the same relationship, the positive and the negative, the 'plus' and the 'minus', are always present.

The situation is even clearer in the model-obstacle* relationship. I admire or even adore my model. At the same time, I hate him or her because they are destroying my life. Here again, the positive and the negative are in me at the same time. Everything, each of the feelings in me, can change to its opposite at any moment. At the same time, both positive and negative feelings are two sides of the same coin. In fact it is love-hate.

There are numerous examples of love-hate relationships: A mother who embraces her child, hoping to smother it at the same time or a lover of a picture who tries to destroy it. At the level of international politics, the relationship of the USA and the USSR during the Cold War was often an all-consuming love-hate relationship.

When there are no structures, only mimesis*, there are only two possibilities in every relationship in which we live. We are either 'one-up' or we are 'one-down'. If we are up we feel happy. When we are one-up we cannot understand those who complain. In fact they are complaining because they are one-down, but we cannot understand it. When we ourselves are one-down, in the same relationship, it is we who feel miserable and depressed.

Yet, because there are no structures, we are happy or miserable about nothing. There is no longer any reality about which we are fighting. There is just winning and losing within the fight itself. This balance can change at any time, the one-up becoming the one-down and we are unable to do anything about it. Much more important still, the absence of any structure* means that we can never know when the fight is over. The whole game is about nothing because there are no longer any values by which to decide anything. In effect, we are free-floating objects without any solid foundation.

As the rivalry increases, we are increasingly prepared to use any tool to win. Ultimately, all human talents and abilities become used for the mimetic game, which is, in the end, always just a power game. Love, sexuality, knowledge, titles, possessions, even religion*, faith* and death itself become instruments in the fight, used by us to win our fights. Nothing matters in itself. In fact everything is degraded. Everything worthwhile, every relationship is used and destroyed. Ultimately it does not matter whether we win or lose. Life itself has no meaning outside the fight and disappears into nothingness.

Structures sought to ensure that we were different. However, rivalry makes us ever more similar. By rivalling with each other, the last remnants of structure* are destroyed. By fighting structures we manage to achieve precisely what we want to avoid. By fighting to be different, fighting to be one-up, we in fact do the same and difference disappears. As long as and as soon as we are fighting to be different, the end result is that we are the same. In this world without structures, there is no way to come to any final conclusion. Being up or being down, doing this or doing that, ultimately amounts to the same thing. The only thing that matters is the winning or losing of the fight which changes all the time and is much too complicated to be controlled by us.

When the fixed points vanish with the structure*, the game becomes an eternal up and down in which we struggle endlessly and which we lose for certain at the very least at the moment of death. When there is nothing objective to win, winning is only the other side of losing. Even after winning over somebody, there is always someone else higher, so that losing follows winning, and the fight goes on. At the very moment when we win we get a foreboding of losing again. Losing may be just around the corner, coming at any moment.

To put it another way, everything becomes relative to its opposite. There is no substantial or real difference. Any object which was the original object of the fight has long since become irrelevant. The fight is merely about the fight and as such is increasingly about nothing.

Everything has meaning only inasfar as it provides help in winning the power-game of the fight. When we are winners, we find ourselves either loving others or despising them . We are one-up, in 'plus'. The lot of losers on the other hand is hatred or alternatively they find themselves adoring others. Losers are one-down, in 'minus'. For winners, religion* is regarded as good or alternatively it is despised as something for weaklings – they don't need such a thing (plus). For some losers, religion* seems worthless. On the other hand, some losers plunge into religion*, becoming the people so despised by Nietzsche – those with the souls of slaves (minus).

In the end love and hate, believing and not believing, winning
and losing, life and death, man and woman, plus and minus become the same, all meaningless except in their use for the fight.
We all end up in chaos.[7]

5. Person and group: Newton's law

Mimesis* between individual people and mimesis* between groups, or between a person and a group, always works in the same way. In all cases, there is always the mimesis* of desire and the consequences remain the same. If we analyse relationships, there is no difference in the mechanisms operating between persons and between groups. Both persons and groups are in temporal and in spatial mimesis*.

Just how far groups are in temporal mimesis* – in mimesis* with their histories – we know from our experience in Ireland, where memories and myths are so important. Because we are always in mimesis*, people, whether on their own or in groups, can only change when the lines of unfreedom and restriction in temporal mimesis* are cut by new experiences in the present – experiences in spatial mimesis*. They can only change through a new relationship. In this way the experience of change, freedom*, is given. New lines of spatial mimesis* expel the old lines of temporal mimesis*, and as a result the old lines are really forgotten. Sometimes, Roman Catholic Irish people meet Protestant Irish people(and the other way around), and they recognise each other for the first time as human beings, the same as they are themselves. At the very moment that they meet in a new way, they forget the old memories which kept them apart .

We sometimes have the impression that groups are more difficult to change because of their complexity. In reality, both groups and persons are extremely complicated. We never actually know most of the complications of each person, in the same way as we ignore most of the complications of mimesis* which constitute the life of the group. For us, the most important difference may be that we have less experience of changing groups and we therefore don't know how to do it.

Newton's law makes an interesting parallel in respect of mimesis*. Newton found that gravity equalled mass divided by the square of the distance between the objects. If we translate the law into mimetic language we get an idea of the different power of different relationships. The force by which we are drawn into mimesis*, and by which others are drawn into mimesis*, with someone or something, is equal to the mass of the mediator (the person with whom I come into mimesis*) divided by the square of the distance from the mediator.

The 'mass' of a mother is very great for her baby, the distance nearly zero and thus the force of the mimesis* for the baby is huge. A crowd is another large mass. We are drawn into mimesis* with it before we know it. On our own we will never convince a crowd unless we are in mimesis* with something else and hence have other possibilities – which again can be seen to constitute a mass for the crowd. A very important person also usually represents great mass. Wishing to discuss something with such a person – while still remaining free to disagree with him – means that we ourselves have to be very free if we are not to be drawn into mimesis* with him. Otherwise we lose, or we end up in a fight .

In fact, every time we try to convince other people, we are in a power game. By far the most hopeful possibility in convincing another is not to try to convince. It is enough to tell the other who we are, who we follow, what is true for us and to leave the other person free to decide whether to go in the same way or not.

6. Culture

The big question is: If human beings are in constant rivalry, how did culture* – the possibility of living together as human beings – develop? How is it possible that we live together without destroying one another? The answer is the scapegoat* mechanism, the possibility we have to scapegoat* other people for all of our problems.

Over and over again, we human beings have succeeded and succeed in getting rid of our responsibility for our mistakes, faults or tricks, by making another person or group of people responsible. In so doing we are certain that the consequences of our actions – havoc, discord and violence – are not our fault, but his or hers. Only if we agree about who is to blame is there a chance of living in culture*. We live in unity agreeing about this, even if ultimately only about this.

Desiring always provoked chaos. At the dawn of culture*, people repeatedly experienced that chaos disappeared and life became possible if one member of the group was held responsible for all of the difficulties which arose, if one person was scapegoated. A long learning process began, leading to the emergence of culture*. Culture* was necessary to prevent desire destroying all the possibilities of life. There are central features of this process which are still vital for our daily lives:

1. *Rites:* Peace came when the scapegoat* was unanimously driven out, and everybody else found peace together. In rites, the original event which ended with the driving out of the scapegoat* is repeated with more or less the same results. A complete rite runs more or less as follows: There is peace of sorts, but that peace is fragile and increasingly so. People begin by making jokes at the cost of others. This stage of the scapegoating* process is represented by comedy. But the situation turns serious. It becomes clearer who the scapegoat* will be. This is the stage of tragedy. Eventually the scene erupts into wild dancing and noise making (all music is ritual, as is all art). Finally the scapegoat* is driven out, killed, done away with and peace comes.

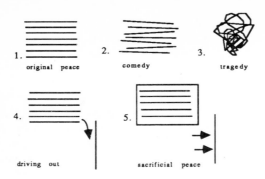

Time too becomes ritualised. The rites were performed at certain times.

There is still considerable ritual in our culture*. Events and times such as Christmas, Easter, carnival, 11th,12th July and even everyday rituals such as shaking hands, funerals, confirmation, marriage and so on are all rites. This is true in the lives of nations, groups, families and separate persons. Even the wearing of a badge is ritual.

Other aspects of ritual continue all the time. As a group we can make fun of a person, so driving him or her out. In general we are not aware of our own rituals. But we are still driving out the unwanted as our ancestors did. In driving out the scapegoat* we are making life possible and at the same time hiding the reality of our lives. We never see what it is of ourselves that we are driving out and wanting to be rid of. The scapegoat* 'carries away' our violence for us. In fact we are always driving out our own violence and the possibility we have for disagreements. We use a man, a woman, a group, a situation or anything to be responsible for our being as we are. Thus we make scapegoats*, called in psychotherapy our identified patients, who are held to be the problem. Our problem in modern culture* is that we can no longer solve our problems in this way. We can only change our problems and make new ones to replace the old ones.[8]

One of the difficulties is that we are always sure that our scapegoats* are not scapegoats*. We are convinced that we are perfectly right in blaming them as the cause of our trouble. This is, in fact, an illusion. When we see other people scapegoating*, we don't accept it. So the really big task is to stop finding other people's scapegoating* and to turn to the much more difficult one of finding our own. Only in this way can we find out what we are doing with other people.

2. *Myths*: Originally the group that drove out the scapegoat* told its story of what happened . They always did this in the form of a myth. But this was never the tale of what really happened. In fact it was always history as seen by the survivors or winners. The scapegoat* was actually no more responsible than everybody else for the chaos between people. In every myth, the story was told that the scapegoat* was solely responsible for the problem. The scapegoat* was deliberately and consciously evil, transgressed all the laws and attempted to, or desired to, destroy our culture*, our way of living and our peace. He was the real, objective, bad person, a real devil. The others, we, were the goodies.

Despite all the changes since these times, we still have our myths – our 'narratives', our personal stories – which we tell about our lives. We need them in order to be a person. Nevertheless, they are mythical. They seldom tell the truth, but rather tell our myth in which the scapegoating* goes on. To put it another way: As long as we live in culture* we can't live with the truth.

We have to make and to fake histories. We have all had the experience of telling stories about our lives while people who know us well smile knowingly. They know that the story is not true and that it is only our story, the story we need to stay ourselves as we think we are, and to have self-respect. Both myths and rites are ways of hiding the truth, although they are beautiful to tell. But every now and then, while telling them, we become aware that we are living in lies, both our own and those of other people.

In myths people are always divided into the good and the bad. Because we are living in this reality, the reality of culture*, we assume these myths to be true. We also always divide people into goodies and baddies. This type of reality is mythical, a lie. However, we now know that as soon as we talk about people as 'bad' we are living in the mythical world. In fact we are hypocrites.

We are also hypocrites when we are moralising to or about others. Moralising means that we are telling others that some people or some person is bad. We hide the truth about ourselves by pointing the finger at others. In moralising there is always a feeling of aggression by which we defend ourselves. Moralising belongs to the world of scapegoating* as well. This is the reason we are all so scared of being moralised to or about. In fact we fear being scapegoated.

We all have the same possibilities of good and bad. The fact that we are each different is not our doing and has nothing to do with merit. Culture* always made sure that people were different so that the possibility of rivalry was reduced and the worst possibilities which are in everybody had no chance to become reality. The more cultural order disappears the more culture* is unable to fulfil its task and the more it becomes a matter of luck whether we end up as a Minister of State or the head of a gang of criminals, a good citizen or a terrorist.

We are not born to be good or bad. Our possibilities emerge in the endless encounters we have in life. In a society in which culture* is disappearing, those who are the most able scapegoaters are the most successful. Any time we succeed we can ask ourselves 'who are our scapegoats*?'

3. *Laws*: Laws also originated as an attempt to prevent desiring, and therefore violence, from returning into society and culture*. They still come most strongly into action when structures are being undermined and culture*, and therefore human life as such, is endangered. The ten commandments (see section 24) were originally religious laws forbidding desire; to desire to be like god, to envy neighbours, the desire to have everything.

4. *Structure*: In order to prevent desire and hence rivalry, everybody had a place in the structure* of the society or the group. Everybody had his or her rights and duties. Leaving your place, desiring the place of another, whether in your own layer of the structure* or in another one, was prohibited. To desire beyond the boundaries of the structure* was forbidden and the prohibition was so accepted, so taken for granted that it was simply part of life, not even a question of conscious obedience. Honour your

parents does not mean love them but rather let them have their own place as parents, do not intrude on their place[9]. Let your boss have his or her own place, don't rival with him or her. The reverse is equally true: Let your workers have their place, honour them and don't rival with them.

Culture* was always built on differences. We have to have differences because only then can we be free of rivalry and life is clear and secure. Myths, rites, laws, and structure* together sought to ensure that differences came into existence and remained or were renewed. In the end all that we need or want to know is that 'they' are different – that Catholics or Protestants are different. Exactly how or why they are different does not necessarily interest us. It may even be dangerous to know because maybe then the differences might fall away.

It is important to be clear that when cultural differences have fallen away, as has happened and is happening now, we can never go back to them as they were. We have to meet and find new ways together.

7. The teaching and learning process

Parents or teachers who are rivalling with a child can teach them hardly anything. In fact, while they are rivalling, they don't really wish to teach anything. The only thing which the child learns from them in this situation is to rival. The child will end up fighting against them, and so the possibility of development and learning will be destroyed. For as long as we are in model-rival* or model-obstacle* relationships no real learning is possible. Furthermore the rivalry destroys the possibility of life, mentioned in Exodus 20:12. Model-rival* and model-obstacle* relationships are a great source of neurosis, the source of all failure in life.

In order to be able to teach and learn we need another relationship, one in which the model is only a model and does not become a rival or an obstacle. In other words, the relationship must be a free one – free of the mimesis* of desire. Relationships can only be free if everybody has their place in them. A father must be a father, a mother a mother and a teacher a teacher, each knowing what that means. He or she must accept the tasks involved and carry the responsibility, committed to and doing the work. The child also has to have his or her rights and duties. We can only find the freedom* to be a father, mother or teacher if we accept the place with all our being.

The model also has the task (and the freedom*) to 'die' as a model. Ultimately this means giving the child or the student the freedom* to go his or her own way. There is no teaching without being what you are in freedom* and without being prepared to 'die'. Equally, there is no learning without being prepared that your parent or teacher will one day 'die' or 'leave', giving you the possibility to go your own way. We can put this into a model as well:

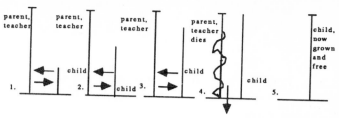

If, instead of freedom*, there is rivalry, then much less or even nothing can be learnt. The child never really grows up and never becomes free because the rivalry with his or her parents continues and the relationship never ends. The result is a life-long bind, the consequence of which is a life-long struggle. This is of interest to all of us, not only to parents and teachers. People will only be free to learn something from us inasfar as we ourselves are free, allowing the other to become free and giving them the freedom* to do as they choose. As soon as we begin to rival with them, by trying to convince them of our own rightness or as soon as we become obstacles for them by showing that we are better or have more insight, everything is lost. We can only be free in our relationships if we return to the model-model relationship. In practice this means that when adults are with children freedom* is given when we return to structure*, and when adults are with adults we return to freedom*, leaving each other free.

8. 'The rise and fall of culture'

For various reasons the old myths, rites, laws and structures are less and less effective. We still have our myths, but increasingly in our society they are reduced to myths shared only with our immediate group, our family or believed only by ourselves. We still have rites and ritual which in many cases are very important for our lives, but hardly any of them are real, functioning rites for the whole society. The 12th of July celebration in Northern Ireland is not a ritual for the whole of society. It is a ritual for only one group, used to drive out the others. Likewise, some of our remaining rites are used to drive out parts of our own people, of our own families and the parts of our own lives which we want to forget.

There are still laws, but mostly we act as though these are only applicable to others. Meanwhile we no longer need to obey them ourselves, for reasons only we understand. There are numerous examples of this: Other people should obey the speed limit, they should pay all their taxes, he should never drink and drive. On the other hand, I have my own legitimate reasons for 'the few occasions' when I am not obeying the law. In this way, the most important remaining function of law becomes to scapegoat* other people, finding them more guilty than myself. We can draw another model trying to show the disappearance of structure*:

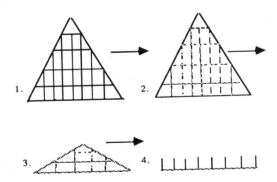

As structure* disappears, competition increases between every-body. In fact, society becomes more and more undifferentiated. In terms of our diagrams, we all end up on one level. Because structure* has disappeared, all clarity in our relationships disap-pears. We cannot live without clarity. So we end up fighting to create our own structure*, a temporary, personal one. The only possibility that appears open to us, whether we are conscious of it or not, is to order the universe we live in after our design. Thus even if we put somebody else or an ideal on top in our system, it remains our system where we retain the power in it. Of course lots of other people are fighting for their own structures. As a re-sult, life becomes an endless round of winning and losing, full of foul and temporary tactical compromises. The predicament which Dostoevsky describes in his novels of the single person who is opposed to everybody else – that I am alone and all the others are together – has become the reality of our life. Everybody is to some degree our rival and enemy.

9. Man – Woman – Marriage – the Family

From the time of our birth, we grow up with other people around us. We become and are who we are by learning from them. This takes place from the beginning of our lives and we always carry the deep imprint of this learning process . For nearly everybody, the first important people were and are our parents.

A married couple are very close to one another both physically and in terms of human relationship. The danger that they rival with one another is thus equally great. Rivalry can only be prevented by differences. When the husband, the wife and the children have their own places, there is a possibility that everybody can live in peace.

Culture* was always very conscious of this. In every society, men and women had their own place, their own rights and duties. Each had their own territory on which the other was not allowed to intrude. They had different languages, even different tools for the same work.

In a model:

Today in our culture*, the structure* is breaking down. There are still many traces of what once was. There are still some words used by boys that girls do not use. Most parents are still aware of their responsibilities to one another and for their children. Nevertheless, rivalry in many places is becoming more and more intense, between husband and wife, between parents and children. Children growing up with rivalling parents rival with them as well. Often they have no other choice if they want to survive other than to rival. Love which was once possible because it was freely given between two people increasingly deteriorates into a power struggle. As in everything else, we love each other only for as long as and whenever the other fits into this game.

Our culture* has become sexist. By this we mean that our gender is no longer a matter of fact. It has become part of the fight which we use against one another. For the form of our lives it no longer matters whether we are man, woman or child. We end up using the fact of our being a man, a woman or a child as part of the fight against the others: women against men, men against women, grown-ups against children and so on. Ultimately, the only thing which matters is power and the possibility of winning over and exploiting the other. We are all caught up in this power game, losing our identity within it and ensuring that the different possibilities we all have become increasingly identical. The only hope we have is to be aware of this fact, and to be conscious of it. Occasionally we may then be able to find ways out, and thus change reality a little bit. In describing this we describe the heart of modern life – the heart of our culture*. There is clearly no way back to any idealised past. At the same time it is clear that we cannot stay in our present situation.

10. Religion

Religion* is the world of the people who do the scapegoating*, the world of the scapegoaters. Religion* is not the same as faith*. We use the word religion* in the sense that cultural anthropology uses it to describe what happens in all cultures. In religion*, the scapegoaters have driven out their scapegoat*, the devil, the one whose presence only meant chaos and who brought chaos by breaking all the rules. Yet the moment he was killed, an incomprehensible peace followed. Miraculously, he gave peace as well; he is a god too.

The origins of religion* and the origins of culture* are the same. In other words, culture* and religion* are the same. It is impossible to be in culture* and outside religion*. Myths, rites, structure* and law are the origin of culture* and the origin of religion*. Our religion* may be all but completely hidden in our culture* – even hidden to ourselves – but this does not alter the reality. For as long as we live in this culture* and in this world, we are living in religion* as well.

Faith*, on the other hand, is a totally different reality from religion*. Faith* is the world of the scapegoats*, of those who are driven out. In a sense, it is the world of religion* turned on its head, as the gospel turns everything on its head! The scapegoats* have recognised that God is not the same as the god of the violent and powerful, the god of religion*, but rather he is the God of the weak.

Religion* and culture* emerged everywhere through violence. We can outline the means by which both emerged. All original groups lived in mimesis* with one another, without a transcendence*. Because the mimesis* of desire became greater and greater, the group fell into destructive violence. Only through the arbitrary choice of a member of the group as the scapegoat* and the subsequent expulsion and concentration of violence onto him was it possible for the group to find peace.

We can show this in a model.

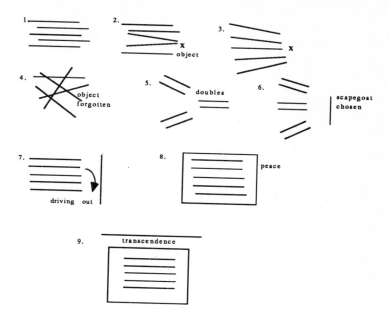

In the course of driving out the scapegoat*, the rest of the community find themselves together, no longer rivalling one another but all looking in the same direction, all looking at the scapegoat*. This is the real source of the peace which descends on the community after the expulsion. Nevertheless, in the myths, the peace is attributed to the special powers of the scapegoat*.

The sacred in culture* and religion* is the totality of all the emotions and feelings, the total of all the experiences which people go through during this sacrificial chaos. This includes the peace which follows the violent expulsion of the scapegoat*. Whenever violence reappears, the feelings re-emerge and we reach, mostly without thinking, for sacrificial solutions. We seek for someone to blame, for scapegoats* to expel once again. There are endless examples of this. The violence of Northern Ireland, with its scapegoating*, is filled with the sacred and the search for the one who is to blame. We find ourselves horrified by the sacred but at the same time we are totally fascinated.

Fascination* is central to the experience of the sacred. Violence always brings fascination*. When we are told about or witness a lynching, we are horrified by it and at the same time we are drawn towards it almost as if by magic. When we see what is happening, it becomes clear that violence and the sacred are the same. Violence draws us into its orbit, because in the violence is the rivalry, the sacrificial chaos. Without really consciously knowing it, we hope that the scapegoat* will be expelled and that peace will come. At the same time the terror inspired by violence never leaves – the terror inspired by the fact that we ourselves might become the scapegoat*, the victim of that violence. Violence like the sacred can destroy us.

Wherever there is violence we find religion* and culture* close by. Escalating violence brings an increasingly desperate search for the scapegoat*. In Northern Ireland, we can see it in the life of the church, which becomes more 'religious' and does more violence. The same mechanism operates in politics, for the terrorist and for us in our own lives. As soon as our thoughts, imagination or deeds become violent we are in the realm of religion*, seeking our scapegoats* and fearing to be made a scapegoat* ourselves. Without knowing it, we are seeking peace in the cultural manner – the old paradoxical manner which is no longer a real possibility.

Culture* and religion* always differentiated between violence which was good and violence which was bad. Bad violence is the violence used to destroy the community by external enemies or by enemies within called criminals. Good violence is the violence of the community preventing or pushing back bad violence.

One of the signs of our time is that the distinction between the two is fading. We are no longer sure that justice is done or even possible in our society. In many places, many of us are no longer sure that the police are serving the law. As a result, violence spreads. Violence increasingly risks provoking more violence whatever the 'reason' for its use. More and more violence becomes just violence, even if it is intended for a culturally 'good' purpose.

After the scapegoat* has been driven out of the community, they are held to be responsible for both the chaos and for the peace which comes about after the expulsion. As a result, the scapegoat* paradoxically becomes both the devil and the god in religion*. The myth says that this was the person who was incredibly bad. It was this person who destroyed the entire community by doing everything that was forbidden in sacred law. As a result, he must be the devil. At the same time, though this is totally incomprehensible, he brought peace. By bringing this good, it must mean that he was god as well.

In effect, the devil, who did both incomprehensible bad and unexpected good, becomes the ruler of our cultural reality. This devil is also the god with whom one must be at peace. At the same time, the god must be feared. His moods of anger and benevolence are totally unpredictable. As long as we fear god or hope that he will help us out of the blue, we too are in the world of religion*. The same is true when we threaten our children with god or with Jesus. We are doing the same thing again when we call our opponents the enemies of god or when we implore god to help us against them. Whenever we live in this sort of world we are in the world of religion*, of violence and of hypocrisy.[10]

To religion* belong structure*, myths, rites and law. Culture* continues to exist through these realities. In many ways, we can be very relieved that parts of these religious realities are still functioning. If they were not, we would all be destroyed by violence and chaos. Nevertheless we can only live within them if our hearts are in the reality of the gospel, never selling ourselves to them.

All of culture* is founded on violence and hypocrisy. Culture's understanding of the truth about itself is a delusion and it is therefore always hypocritical. In reality, the scapegoat* is no worse than we are. But we need to be convinced that he is bad, otherwise our culture*, our life, does not 'work'. As long as we live in culture* we are caught up in double-binds. Part of us wants to be honest and truthful about ourselves but deep in our hearts we know that we are not and even more, we don't even want to be.

Throughout the ages of culture's existence, people have not really known what they are doing. The myths of religion* were 'simply' true. People scapegoated with a clear conscience.[11] Now that hypocrisy has begun to be revealed after all the centuries, it is no longer possible to shut our ears to what Jesus is actually saying to us. We begin to see ourselves for what we are, seeing ourselves with the eyes of Jesus. We can start to see that we are misusing everybody and misusing nature. We hate knowing this and we go on. We know that we are destroying ourselves and the future of our children. Worse still we know that everything that we try within our culture* at best does not work and at worst has the opposite effect to that intended. Here again, the plus and the minus are the same (see section 4). We belong to this culture* and are enslaved by it. At the same time, we know that we can't continue and wish to escape it.

From the outset, the christian church became increasingly religious. It belonged more and more to culture* and preached the devil-god against people in the community and against others. It used this god against enemies inside and outside the church. Soon, various churches identified themselves with their nation and with their group, so becoming rivalling groups, rivalling in and with the world. Each group fought , for the fulfilment of the laws. They used the concepts of this world to defend themselves and, they thought, the gospel.

We do not need to stand in judgement over this. By joining with culture*, the church also saved Western Europe during the Dark Ages when the Western Roman Empire disintegrated. It thus performed a huge cultural task. It also saved the text of the gospels so that we can read them and live from them today. The churches remain very religious, exactly the same as we all are. At the same time it remains true that the gospel is the reality on which the church is built and it knows, as we can know, that there is only a way to the future in the gospel.

Culture* is religion*. Because culture* is disintegrating, religion* is fading away. Everything becomes more ambivalent and more uncertain. This fact does not alter the unity of culture* and religion*. Nor does it change the reality that life is founded on religion*. All that happens is that this fact becomes more and more hidden. Increasingly we each act as though we don't have any religion* at all. Everything in society becomes more and more fragmented.

One of the most profound consequences is that both the state and the church, both more or less religious institutions, are crumbling away. They try desperately to stay in power for reasons which are both subjectively and objectively good . In reality, both state and church have become increasingly ornamental or they fade away with religion* itself.

Ultimately whether we precisely understand what is happening in society or not is secondary. Most important of all is that we seek new ways to go.

11. Transcendence, Freedom and Structure in Culture

Any group which once lived within a traditional religion* lived with a *transcendence*. This means that there was a reality which was above the group, 'up in the air', beyond manipulation by the group or any member of the group and ruling or confining the group as a whole. Every member of the group was in mimesis* with this transcendence*. This is the god or the gods. Everything which is sacred is so because it belongs to the god. The structure* of society, (laws, rules, everything in fact which was common to everybody, which everyone obeyed) belonged to the god and was sacred. Disobedience meant sacrilege and for a long time meant the death penalty for the transgressor. Anybody who did not obey the transcendence* could not belong to the group. He was too dangerous for a number of reasons.

Living with others within this transcendence* means that everyone has their place, their rights, duties and freedom* to relate to everybody. Because everybody knows what their place is, this applies universally. The whole world is yours because the whole world is the world under this transcendence*. When we speak of the whole world here we mean the whole world as far as we recognise it to be the world, the world in which our transcendence*, our god, is god. For a long time, the whole world meant only the world of the group. This was true even for the Greeks, where only the Greek world counted as the world. In a diagram we can picture this.

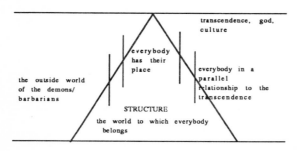

In culture*, there is a vertical transcendence* which is valid for everybody. Nobody in the society can rival with the transcendence* because it is out of reach. The same is true for relationships which are structurally separated. Another way to describe this is to say that there is *external* mediation*. Mediation* means that the model transmits or 'mediates' a desire to the person who is in mimesis* with him or her. When I see my model and desire what he desires, I have his desire mediated to me. External mediation* means that my model does not live in the same world as me. This is the result of distance, either geographical or in time, or both. As a result, my model does not rival with me. When the transcendence* is completely vertical, it means that there is no rivalry between us.

Structure* under a transcendence* abolished rivalry. This is or was true for relationships with the gods and equally for the relationships of parents and children, authorities and citizens, bosses and workers, ministers, priests and members of the community.

Transcendence* did not mean that you had to obey everything. It meant, however that disobedience was recognised by you as disobedience. Obedience and disobedience were clearly separate. As such disobedience was undertaken in freedom*. You knew that you had to disobey. This is different from disobedience out of rivalry and unfreedom in which we do not know where we are going or why we are disobeying. Ultimately we do not even recognise that we are disobeying.

Real vertical transcendence* means that there is no rivalry between the person and the transcendence*. There is external mediation*. Not all external mediation* has a completely vertical transcendence*. If we are following an ideal person, whether real or imaginary, the person may indeed remain unreachable and out of rivalry. Nevertheless, although he or she does not rival with us, we can rival with them. Unlike free relationships, the transcendence* is no longer vertical. In terms of our diagrams, transcendence* becomes 'oblique', 'skewed' or 'deviated'.

Oblique or deviated transcendence* always appears when a real or fantasised human being is being treated as a god. There are numerous examples of this in literature. Amadis of Gaul is a god for Don Quixote, while the Parisian women are goddesses for Emma Bovary in Flaubert's novel. In both cases, life is lived in the transcendence* of the gods but the transcendence* is not complete. Deviated transcendence* already has to do with desire and rivalry, a desire to be somebody else. This desire to be another, to have the being of another, we call metaphysical desire.

Deviated transcendence* always means that both the world and our freedom* have become smaller than under vertical transcendence*. Large parts of the world are unimportant and uninteresting to us because we are focussed only on our desires. When we are desiring, our focus is always more and more on our desires. Hence our world becomes smaller.

When our external mediator is an ideal person, we rival with them. We try to be as good, as courageous or as beautiful as them, which is the same as saying that we wish to be better than them. They have become transcendent for us, showing us the world or the reality in which we wish to live. All the other possibilities of the world have become unimportant to us. The possibilities of our lives are now restricted to those given to us by the relationship to our ideal. We can no longer see the world around us but rather see it through the eyes, the fantasised eyes, of our model. Their world has become the only worthwhile world. Because we are in such rivalry with our model, totally together with them, we are closed in in that world. As a result we fail to see the real world and we do many foolish things because we no longer really see the world in which we are operating. Exactly in this way, Don Quixote and Emma Bovary make fools of themselves to those watching them.

The world is reduced in a number of ways. Although we remain physically in the whole world, we can now see only certain aspects of it. This was what happened to Don Quixote trying to be like Amadis of Gaul.

Don Quixote travelled through Spain on his quest. He was also full of good intentions. Likewise, we might try to be as pious as we think Jesus was. So often, we use him as the great example, the ideal to be followed. Insodoing we are in fact trying to become as good or as pious as he is in our pious, rivalrous dreams. So we go about trying to convert everybody, taking away their freedom*. There is a long tradition in the Christian churches of consciously trying to be pious, of trying to become like the Jesus of our fantasies. It may therefore be hard to understand that the consequences of this form of mimesis* are deeply damaging. Even though our oblique transcendence* mean that we still have a lot of space in which to move, we are damaging our neighbours and destroying ourselves, despite the fact that it is all done with the best intentions. It remains a game of pride. How can we ever become as good as this non-desiring man when we try to do so by desiring? Pride always destroys others. We will never make it on our quest to be as good as Jesus. It is pious snobbery, because we are pretending to be better than others while in our innermost heart we know that it isn't true. Snobbery destroys us.[12]

Nevertheless, there is still space to move in this relationship. We can still move around, we can take decisions, there is some structure* even if we do use it to our own ends. The next development results in the world becoming smaller in every sense. Geographically the only world which matters is the world in which our hero or heroine lives – Paris, the Hollywood of the stars, or whatever. We become convinced that only the model's life is worth living. This is our fate if we follow people whose lives belong very much to a particular place. We are closed up in their world in every way and we lose nearly all contact with reality. We, the desiring people, are nevertheless more convinced than ever that we are living in or are hunting after a higher reality than that in which everybody else lives.

In fact we are not living in the situation in which we actually are, nor are we really living elsewhere. There is still some structure*, still some room for manoeuvre but we destroy it increasingly because we are always seeking to shape reality to the form of our dreams and always failing. In our rivalry with our external mediator – striving to be them, full of metaphysical desire – we now try to become external mediators for all those around us. We tell them that they should be like we are. As a result they begin to rival with us, eventually scapegoating* us or we them. Life becomes more and more meaningless. In a series of diagrams we can see this process.

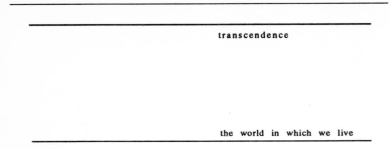

1. Real transcendence*, God, goes everywhere with us. He stays with us, wherever we are, giving us freedom* in all places at all times.

2. This changes already if our transcendence* is an ideal, be it justice, a sense of duty or whatever. We can picture this change in another diagram:

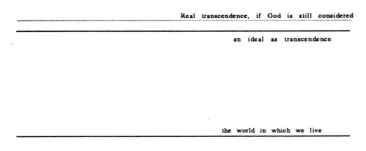

We can still move freely everywhere, but we are no longer really free. The world has to fulfil the requirements of our ideal. We see reality and we try to transform it in accordance with our ideal. We ourselves are subject to laws which we now impose on everybody and everything around us. Of course this becomes more tyrannical the 'lower' the level of the ideal: the interest of my country, of my class, of my family, of myself, of 'science' or even of my own career and so on. When we try to be like Jesus, he is an ideal of this sort.

3. Don Quixote moves around in a smaller world. It can be pictured like this:

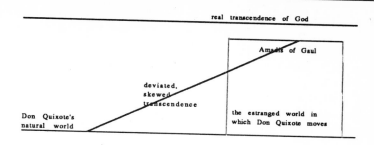

Don Quixote still assumes a real transcendence*. At his death, he returns to it, to God. But for as long as he is transfixed by Amadis, this real transcendence* does not play a real role. For Don Quixote, Amadis is above him. Amadis is elsewhere and as such he is external. The whole of reality becomes distorted because of Don Quixote's skewed vision.

Don Quixote is still living in reality but this reality has to obey his dreams, his ideals of how things should be. He wants to be very noble, as noble as Amadis himself. In fact he wishes to outdo Amadis. In trying to achieve this he destroys everything and everybody he meets. Nobility is only possible in structure*, when we stay where we are, or under real transcendence* when we are really serving in love. Otherwise we end up making nonsense.

4. For Madame Bovary in Flaubert's novel, transcendence* is lower still.

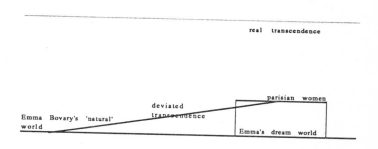

Madame Bovary still knows a little bit about real transcendence*. In her anguish, she tries to find some inner support in the church.

But in fact this is only memory. Her functioning transcendence* is the Parisian women and the demi-monde of Paris. This world is so close and yet still unattainable. She becomes totally estranged from the world in which she actually lives. Nothing in her world matches her dreams. She destroys it much more thoroughly than did Don Quixote. There is no going back for her, as there still was for him. In her mimetic madness she destroys herself and her family.

The last phase in the descent from transcendence* is internal mediation*, where all external mediation* has broken down and we are all rivals and idols for one another, each other's model-obstacle*s. Our integrity as human beings stems from an external relationship which protects us from rivalling with everyone we meet. As soon as transcendence* has disappeared and we have no being outside of our immediate relationships we have no internal stability. We are in fact as many different people as the number of people we meet as a result of being in mimesis* with everyone. Ultimately we are permanently in chaos, in rivalry with everyone we meet. We no longer have the possibility of finding a real way for ourselves.

Structure* in the old sense existed and could exist only because people acknowledged transcendence*. Now that transcendence* has disappeared, structure* no longer has any authority. Instead, we use our views of the old transcendence* as weapons against each other in an eternal powerfight in which we try to build our own structure* which we control. In this powerfight we are 'at the top of the pyramid'. However, as the process accelerates, with everybody fighting, the structure* is destroyed at an increasing rate. The same is true of laws, morality and all rules. They all apply to others and are to be administered by us.

Without transcendence* we are many 'personalities' – as many personalities as there are important people and groups in our lives. Sociologists refer to this as the 'roles' people have to 'play', that they live with and in. This is indeed how it appears. Ultimately, however, there is nothing beyond the roles. Each role is the reality of us in each situation. In fact we are split up and centreless. There is no longer any real direction in our lives. Inasfar as there is direction, it is forced upon us and we can only see it in retrospect. Everything is apparently possible, but at the same time we are unable to be anything. The alienation which Marx saw as the predicament of the workers in a capitalist society has become everybody's predicament in modern culture*.

One of the results of this cultural process is that, increasingly, we prefer to remain voyeurs, onlookers doing nothing. The rivalry is now so intense, and taking part is so dangerous, that we prefer to watch from the sidelines. In this context, television is manna from heaven. The voyeur is made into a responsible citizen. Much of our excitement in life, especially in the realm of sex and violence, comes from looking on. We can take part in the rivalry and have the excitement, but we do so without running any immediate risks. Our feelings overwhelm us but there are no consequences except that we are using up our lives and possibilities without any result. Ultimately, life itself becomes senseless.

In the end, the world and its opportunities disappear completely. We have become the slave or prisoner of every relationship we live in. We even make a virtue out of it, calling it 'living for the moment'. History and all real knowledge disappear because they are not 'worthwhile' amidst the excitement. We know everything and nothing and our freedom* is gone.

In reality today we live in all these different worlds, from the structured to the chaotic, at different times. The direction of everybody's life is that there is less and less transcendence* and more and more internal mediation*. Our lives, our families and our countries have become more and more ungovernable. Everybody simply seeks what they define as their own interests.

12. External and internal mediation: Another angle

Mediation* of desire occurs between single people, between groups and between single people and groups who are in mimesis* with each other. For a long time in culture*, external mimesis* was by far the most important reality in life. In external mediation*, the person who transmits the desire, the mediator, has a different position in society from that of the person who adopts the desire. In effect, the mediator cannot be reached by the people who mimetically adopt his desire. It is important to remember again that mimetic desire is very often unconscious. Those who desire mimetically can rival with the model, the mediator, but the mediator does not rival with his or her imitators. They are not desirable enough for him or her to do that. In the same way, we can always rival with God, but God will never rival with us. A servant could rival with his master, but the master never rivalled with his servant for as long as the differences were clear. As long as the mediator belongs to a different world from that of his or her imitators, reciprocal rivalry does not happen.

The most fundamental external mediation* is the mimesis* with God. God, the God of faith* does not desire and is not violent. This is the distinction between him and the gods of religion* who are, and do, both. In mimesis* with God, we become free of desire and of violence. We become free. We remain in mimesis*, the mimesis* of freedom*, but we are freed of the enigma of culture*, the mimesis* of desire.

Another form of external mediation* is still in some families, which are in a sense old-fashioned. In these families there is still structure*. The parent in his or her position is unreachable for the child. The parent is still a model. There is no rivalry. The same is the case for a teacher who is free with the pupils and as a result is unreachable for them. He mediates his knowledge which the pupils learn in mimesis* with him. There is external mimesis* and there is a fruitful learning process. With the disappearance of external mediation* and its replacement with rivalry, the learning process is destroyed.

Things become much more risky when we choose a historical person as our mediator or a living personality who is outside of our world. Another possibility might arise if we choose a mythical character or a character out of a novel as our model, our ideal, our idol. In all of these cases there is no reciprocal rivalry with all the chaos which comes from that. However, those who choose the external mediator as their model – their idol – can easily rival with them as we saw with Don Quixote and Emma Bovary. (See section 11)

When we begin rivalling with external models, culture* has already begun to decay. For as long as the decay is not complete, culture* prevents rivalry. Desiring and rivalry are simply prohibited. The Ten Commandments prohibit rivalling with God and also with our parents. This is the background to the commandments against making images of God and the duty to honour our parents. When external mediation* is working, there is order in life and the absence of rivalry makes sure that everybody has his or her place. Only in the late stages of European culture* did rivalry with the external mediator really spread and become a problem. Don Quixote was written in the transition from the sixteenth to the seventeenth centuries. Pietism was widespread in Europe during the seventeenth and eighteenth centuries and Madame Bovary was written in the mid-nineteenth century.

External mediation* is about freedom*. Everybody has their place. The meaning and content of movements are all clear. Even when the rivalry with the external mediator begins, a certain freedom* remains. For as long as there is an external mediator we can still confess to one another who our idols are. This becomes impossible when mediation* is internal. A certain freedom* to choose between doing something or not doing it remains. We can still stop for a while or relinquish our ideal entirely.

At the same time, once we begin to rival in external mediation*, very much is destroyed or made impossible. We do mad things, often at the cost of ourselves or at a cost to others. Others have to adapt themselves to us in order to accommodate our ideals. If we have to change life before we can live it, then we become violent from the outset.

The same happens to our external mediators. We are no longer able to see them as they really are. Instead, we see them glorified, bathed in divine light. Don Quixote's Amadis de Gaul had nothing to do with any human being. The Parisian women in Madame Bovary's imagination had nothing in common with the poor creatures who actually existed. In exactly the same way, the Jesus of the pietists is their Jesus, not Jesus himself. We can again try to show this in a diagram.

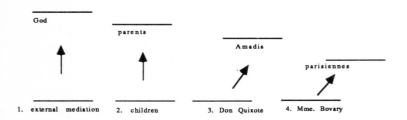

1. external mediation   2. children   3. Don Quixote   4. Mme. Bovary

These are all examples of external mediation*. The first ,when transcendence* is vertical, is without rivalry. The others, where there is rivalry from one side, show a oblique transcendence*. Of course rivalry with God is possible, but as soon as this happens we are rivalling with the gods of religion*. We can rival with our parents as well. For as long as the parents don't react and stay free it doesn't matter that much. If the parents react, then both parents and children disappear into internal mimesis*. In fact, there are no longer parents and children, there is only a fighting bunch of people. At the same time, these parents become devil-gods for their children, over whom they have to win.

In internal mimesis*, both structure* and transcendence* have disappeared. We have become our own law. Nothing separates us any longer from each other. We are irretrievably at the mercy of desire and the inevitable rivalry and model-obstacle* relationships. This is true for all of us and it moves between us, each in mimesis* with the other. Life is full of excitement and full of tension but at the same time it is also full of anxieties. Furthermore, it is full of feelings; feelings of success, feelings of being worthless and feelings of emptiness. Ultimately, freedom* has disappeared.

I am fascinated by you because of what you have and who you are. I have no real choices. I am a prisoner of my own desiring and I cannot escape the desire.

Because we are all in the same situation, all seeking the same, I have to hide the fact that I am desiring and hide the object of my desire even from myself. I have to hide the fact that I desire what you desire or that I follow you. All the time, I have the fantasy that you are following me. In this way I attempt to keep some form of self-respect, but the reality is always the reverse. Sometimes, I hide the reality of desire so well that I am oblivious to it. I even become outraged and indignant when my desiring is pointed out to me. I blush. I protest my innocence and accuse the others of desiring. In fact I am scapegoating* the other person in order to hide myself behind him or her.

As soon as we are in internal mediation* it is impossible for us to be honest about who we are following or what we are desiring and seeking. If we were to be honest, we would make fools out of ourselves and certainly lose. Culture* is by definition based on hypocrisy. Once structure* and transcendence* have disappeared, the hypocrisy becomes personal rather than cultural, subjective rather than objective. We all become personally hypocritical.

Because of the disappearance of structures, we have seen a long process by which external mediation* has been affected by rivalry, albeit unilateral rivalry. Increasingly, the differences on which culture* was built and which culture* at the same time maintained, are disappearing. We are now able to move everywhere: horizontally and vertically, geographically and socially. The mass media abolish differences in time and space, bringing impressions from all times and all places into our living rooms each day, with all the excitement and fascination* which belongs to that. The possibility of there being external mediation* is disappearing. Everything is increasingly internal to our world.

What remains are caricatures. Our external mediators sometimes become tyrants or else they go to pieces. Stalin is an example of a tyrant, Hitler an example both of a tyrant and of a man who went to pieces. Many pop stars, surrounded by thousands of fans, end up rivalling with the image their fans have of them and destroy themselves. They become estranged from the reality of themselves, because their fans do not see them as they are. In the end the image of the pop star in the eyes of his or her fans is no more real than Madame Bovary's idolisation of the Parisian women. But Madame Bovary had an advantage. The women were safe from her and vice versa. This is not true of popstars or filmstars and their fans today. Often they come into mimesis* with their fans and they try to be what their fans desire them to be, gods. This must be one of the reasons why there is so often a religious atmosphere around pop music. The star becomes a model-obstacle*, even for the singer himself. So often, many end up in drugs, alcohol, debts, murder or suicide.

Maybe we feel ourselves above all of this. In fact this is further proof that we too are part of the game. This is another example of a negative reaction being the same as participation, the minus being the same as the plus. In saying that we are above it all, we again act as though we are stronger than this whole world.

In internal mediation* the fighting of everybody against everybody goes on and on. There are no structural limits to the rivalry. We continually come into model-obstacle* relationships, making relationships in which we put people up onto a pedestal, adoring them, making them gods. At the same time, we make sure that we are on pedestals, are adored, are gods. We never are who we appear to be. Appearance and reality diverge, until we no longer know what reality is.

As soon as we agree to be gods for others or for ourselves, we also agree to be devils. In religion*, being a devil belongs to being a god, for all the gods were originally scapegoats*.

13. Hypocrisy and victimisation

In the gospels, we see Jesus talking to the pharisees many times. The pharisees were respectable people who did their utmost to be pious, to be good. Culturally speaking, they were certainly above average. Nevertheless Jesus accuses them of being hypocrites. They deny it of course. They admit that their fathers were hypocrites; they persecuted the prophets. But the pharisees are sure that would never do anything like that . Jesus' response is that this very attitude shows them to be hypocrites. Their fathers may have scapegoated the prophets but they are scapegoating* their fathers. All the time they scapegoat* their fathers they are in fact exactly like them.

In everyday language a hypocrite is somebody who is consciously pretending to be better than he in fact is. We are mostly wrong to assume that hypocrisy is conscious. Indeed, if someone is deliberately feigning they are no longer really a hypocrite – they are cheaters and deceivers. In the gospel hypocrites certainly don't know what they are doing.

This unconscious, and nevertheless real, hypocrisy is what Jesus is teaching the pharisees and what he is teaching us. Whenever we claim to be a better person than somebody else, whenever we compare ourselves to somebody, we are hypocrites. This remains true even if we say that somebody else is better than us, though it may appear to be less damaging. In this case we are negative hypocrites, but hypocrites nonetheless. Once again, the plus and the minus are the same.

Hypocrisy is the foundation of culture*. There is no culture* without hypocrisy. Myths, which are always hypocritical, are the cultural stories which hide the scapegoating*. Myths are not confined to culture*. We all have our stories about our lives, our narratives, in which we hide those parts which we don't want others to know. In these stories we are always driving out parts of reality, scapegoating*, although most of the time we are not conscious of it. Hypocrisy and scapegoating* are in fact the same. It is therefore not surprising that hypocrisy is one of the most important themes of the gospel. Culture* is built on hypocrisy. The scapegoat* who was and is the same as us is no more guilty than we are. He is not a devil, nor a god, even though we may still believe it.

In a culture* which still has elements of external mediation* there is 'objective hypocrisy', a hypocrisy which is shared by everybody without knowing it. While we are living within this culture* we are all hypocrites, participating in it, using its facilities. We may never know that it is built on hypocrisy. Because culture* and religion* are founded on hypocrisy, we are all hypocrites for as long as we live in culture*. Culture* itself conceals our hypocrisy and we are not lying when we protest that we are not hypocrites. We need Jesus to show us that we are indeed hypocrites. When others try to tell us we feel scapegoated and become afraid. They are in fact hypocrites themselves.

Culture* is a lie. In culture*, in religion*, the scapegoat* is a very bad person, which, in fact, is not true. The scapegoat* was and is as good and as bad as we are. Being children of culture*, we do culture's work without thinking. We are killers, as we always were and are in culture*, acting as though we are the good people and others are bad. Jesus is very straightforward about this.[14]

The realisation that the scapegoat* is no better or worse than we ourselves are turns everything upside down. In many ways it is so disastrous for our lives, that we can hardly grasp it, let alone imagine the consequences for the manner in which we are in this world and live in it. Jesus says: As soon as you say that somebody is 'bad' you are scapegoating* them, making a difference between them and you which is founded only on the fact of your making it. By saying that 'he or she is bad', there is the everpresent implication that I am better or not as bad, so placing myself firmly on the side of the 'goodies' . Insodoing, I am in fact driving out my own bad sides and placing them on the other.[15] It is true that this has gone on since the foundation of culture*. It is also true that it made culture* possible but countless people suffered through it.

Jesus is always on the side of those who suffer and pay the cost for our 'decent' life. He tells us that we are hypocrites as well. Our scapegoats*, all those who we call bad, have exactly the same possibilities as we have. They are not innately bad. 'Innate badness' does not exist. Without doing anything consciously, we actually make sure that they do wrong, because we need our wrongdoers to live in the security of knowing that we are good. Thereby we have our peace. Like all hypocrites, we never really know what we are doing.

For a long time now hypocrisy has been a personal matter. Instead of objective hypocrisy we are now subjective hypocrites. Now we know about hypocrisy in general. Modern people like ourselves move in circles of hypocrisy and we always try to defend ourselves from its power. We deny that the cause of our own difficulties is ourselves. We find scapegoats*, but still there is a deep knowledge in our hearts that we are playing a horrible game, which only makes us more desperate to find better, more effective scapegoats*. As a result, we scapegoat* the scapegoaters.

The fact that we know about our own hypocrisy makes us more defensive and worse hypocrites. We are so busy defending ourselves that we use the words scapegoaters and scapegoats* all the time, always hinting at others.[16] We know that those in prison and in mental hospitals are actually no worse than us. We just had more luck. Once again, in the face of this knowledge, we become more desperate to be sure that they are bad or mad. We demand higher penalties. At last we have arrived at the point that the pharisees were at in the time of Jesus. We know about our own hypocrisy because Jesus speaks to us.

Hypocrisy and victimisation belong together. Hypocrites, we, always victimise even without knowing it. We victimise others, nature, things, part of our history or of ourselves. For as long as objective hypocrisy reigns things go smoothly within culture*. Peace, cultural peace, is retained. As we move into internal mediation* and rivalry, the hypocrisy becomes subjective and the rivalry worsens. We continue the scapegoating* but there is no longer peace. We can no longer rid ourselves of the scapegoat*. The devil who we try to blame and cast out comes back into our heart. Although we still have many twists and turns, life ends in chaos.

14. The desire to be: Metaphysical desire

It is now becoming clear that our being as we are is not the result of something inherent, something fixed and independent. At birth, we are only possibility. There may be endless possibilities in our lives and what we are and become is not fixed or predetermined. We are still possibilities. We become who we are through mimesis* with our parents, teachers, relatives, siblings, friends or neighbours, culture* and everything which is around us both in space and in time. Through mimesis* with our parents and with all the other people we have the possibility to meet God. When they are with him, they bring him to us. If things are going well we have some external mimesis* in our lives.

A new-born child gets its being by being in mimesis* with people who are, people who know they have a place and have their inner security. They also bring us into a relationship with God, a vertical transcendence* which makes them free. As always and everywhere we depend on others for everything, for our very being. (see section 1)

We become particular people by being in external mediation*. We become free when the human mediators 'die' as mediators and eventually return in a new capacity. Our parents or our teachers 'die' as upbringers and return as adults, and they still have a place in our life.

In all the mimesis* in which we live from our birth, in all of the relationships in which mimesis* takes place, we seek an ultimate, all-encompassing relationship in which we can live. Not only do we get the form of our life through mimesis* we get our life itself. Not living in a relationship means not to exist at all. The trust that I am a constant being, that I have ongoing consistency, means in reality that I live in a relationship which gives me that constant being which enables me to live with inner peace. As a result, we all crave for relationships, craving ultimately for the last relationship with eternity.

For people for whom culture* is still a reality, all of this is taken for granted, without thinking about it or doubting it. Everything happens in an ordered manner without anybody doing anything for it. Parents and children live in an external mediation* with God, with culture*. The children live in external mediation* with the parents. There is no rivalry. The parents know that they are and so the child is. Through the years, passing through rites of passage, the child becomes a culturally independent being, an adult.

Everything changes when culture* collapses. The parents, like everybody, end up in rivalry with everybody and everything. They no longer have a certain being of their own. They rival with God, with culture* and with each other. From the start they destroy the external mediation* with the child, because they rival with the child. Alternatively, they may desire for their child, which is another form of rivalry, asking their child to succeed where they failed. As a result the child can have no security. In the position of being the weakes from the beginning, it is brought up in rivalry, without a chance to be. We all end up craving being and being unable to achieve it.

We are only secure in and sure about our being when we know that it is founded on somebody of whose existence we are certain and who has the power to give existence. Ultimately, we know this without questioning, without doubt or without being conscious that we know. In being together with this being, being in mimesis* with God, we know that we exist and we are sure of our being.[17] Our personal relationships no longer offer us that security. All our unsure relationships merely increase our insecurity. We have lost God, the God of the gospel or the god of religion* or a mixture of both. In any case, in the process of the decline of culture*, many people have lost him.

To be in our disintegrating culture*, we desperately need God or a god. Having lost him, we move to other gods. We have so many examples of these: politicians, football stars, TV stars, band leaders, friends or people whom we admire . We both make them into gods and we enter rivalry with them, trying to get what they have or at least we imagine that they have: being. This has even entered our language: famous people are 'somebody', other people are 'nobody'. We try to take what we think they have – being – and become what they are – gods. To have being. To be.

As we lose all transcendence* and turn to internal mediation*, desire is no longer about having, although it may look like it. Instead, it is about being. We want the things which our model desires, because we wish to have his or her very being. Through the apparent desire for the object, we actually desire the being of the other. The more heightened the state of rivalry, the less important is the original object of desire. Increasingly it is about the being of our rival. We can put this into another diagram.

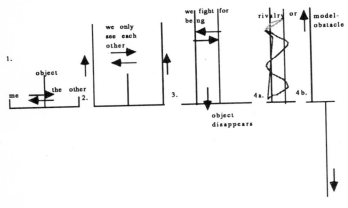

The object very quickly falls into irrelevance. Behind it comes the face of the god whose being we desire. At the same time it is the face of the devil because he will prove to be our model-obstacle* fighting against us for his own being and to have ours. He is our devil-god.

Now that religion* is fading away, we are desperately seeking gods. In fact, we are making gods. As Scheler said, 'men have either a God or an idol'. Because all transcendence*, every reality which is greater or higher than we are and which gives direction to our lives, is waning, God, the gods are disappearing. Ultimately in our search, the only possibility left is that we make gods out of one another. As a result, in mimesis*, we make gods out of ourselves. This desire to be we call metaphysical desire.

All of our attempts to make gods out of one another cannot work.

As a result, we become more and more desperate. In internal mediation*, the rivalry becomes ever greater and increasingly destructive. In this world without God or gods, we fight with and against one another for the being of the other. In our metaphysical desire we are capable of destroying the other and their being, to have the being ourselves. It is one of the aspects of the hopelessness of our world. We are aimlessly drifting vagabonds in our lives. In the end, we do not even have a world.

15. Our scapegoat mechanism

Once the scapegoat* mechanism was the mechanism of the whole group. It had many varieties, often very complex, which were valid for the whole nation. The mechanism established internal peace by driving out violence with violence. The mechanism resulted in structures which gave space, room for everybody in their own place. It also gave freedom*. It was, and as far as it still exists is, a cultural freedom*. This freedom* is founded on the scapegoat* mechanism and therefore founded on hypocrisy. The freedom* was and is institutional freedom* with its clear rights and duties. It was space within strict boundaries but space nevertheless.

The scapegoat* mechanism is the heart of religion*. This mechanism no longer works. The religious system cannot cope with an increasingly complicated reality. The gospel message actually hardened hypocrisy when used as part of of religion* and culture*. Many people felt more self-righteous than ever. Nevertheless, it simultaneously broke down the system. More importantly still, it is no longer possible to fully rid ourselves of our scapegoat*. Whether the scapegoat* is the USSR or South Africa, our partner or our child or whoever our 'baddie' is, we nevertheless have to live with them. The strangest part of this reality is that, ultimately, we decide to keep our scapegoat*, not actually wanting to be rid of them. If our child or partner is ever 'healed' then we are left with the difficulties ourselves. Once we get rid of our original scapegoat* we often have to look for a new one, and that might be ourselves.

Today the world is becoming a 'global village', and, at the same time, it is breaking up into ever smaller units. Although there are of course still differences, things are becoming more and more similar throughout the world. People and groups, whole nations in fact, have no constant or fixed existence and now many are drifting through one another, the only constant being the fight for one-upmanship. The scapegoat* mechanism is everywhere. In

Northern Ireland we still have our scapegoats*, the catholics or the protestants. We have scapegoats* within our communities. Insofar as structure* has broken down we have scapegoating in marriages and in families. Wherever it is, it is a tragedy. Yet we cannot get rid of our scapegoats. As a result we live in a vicious circle where we drive out our problems but they come in again through the back door. In fact, just by trying to get rid of them, by scapegoating*, we are increasing our difficulties.

The scapegoat* mechanism is now everywhere, and we are all afraid that we might be made the scapegoat* whether of our family, of our colleagues, of our group. In fact we scapegoat* others like mad in order to avoid being made the scapegoat* ourselves. The whole situation is made worse because we are only beginning to become aware that we are scapegoating* and when we are scapegoating*. As soon as we are aware of it, it becomes a trick. The truth of what Jesus says on the cross applies to all of us: We do not know what we are doing. Often the scapegoats* are similarly unaware of what is happening. They too play the game in order to prevent chaos, very often suffering without knowing why.

Of one thing we can be certain: We are scapegoating* any time we seek the cause of our difficulties outside of ourselves, in others. Any time we assert that someone else did wrong, is bad or is guilty we are scapegoating*. Every time we label people, we are scapegoating*. There are so many examples of this; describing people as 'bad' or 'good', or as 'superstitious', saying that somebody is 'a heathen', that they will never learn, that they are immoral or that they are always trying to turn things to their own advantage. In fact we are driving out aspects of ourselves which we don't like. Children often say to their parents 'You are exactly the same as you say I am.' This is a golden rule.

We can put this another way. Scapegoating* belongs to the romantic world in which there are good people – the scapegoaters, us – and there are bad people – the scapegoated, them. Here, as everywhere, the gospel turns everything upside down. The sin which Jesus is fighting against is hypocrisy. The scapegoaters, we, are always hypocritical in believing that we are good people. In the gospel, Jesus is always with the scapegoated, the people made bad by the scapegoaters. He is not with the good people. The gospel is not interested in good and bad. Were it possible to side with the scapegoaters, the gospel would become part of religion* and lose its own message. God gives his sun and rain to both the good and the bad . God is not with people who think that they are good, thereby scapegoating* others and making them bad.

I am no better than any other human being. I have exactly the same possibilities as any other person has, even if he or she appears evil to me. When I recognise evil in the other, I am recognising myself. The so-called evil of the other in fact shows me my own possibilities. It can never make me proud but can only serve to make me humble. This is true of our friends, of people far away and even of monstrous political opponents.

In myths, the scapegoat* is always the person who broke all the rules, who did everything which was forbidden, and destroyed culture*. Everybody who breaks the rules is an incarnation of the scapegoat* who has to be driven out in order to restore peace again. Amongst others, prisoners, those who broke the prohibitions, are our scapegoats*.

Terrorists are very able scapegoaters, as we all are. Terrorists are always in model-obstacle* relationships. Consciously or unconsciously, they also seek to become the great important scapegoat* who is sacrificed to save his people, dying that others might be 'set free'. At the same time, terrorism tries to provoke chaos, out of which will come the ritual mechanism and therefore the new order. After the victory everyone will know that the terrorist's enemy, now driven out, really was bad. In all of this complexity, the terrorist seeks to drive out the scapegoat*, thus saving his people and creating a new world. All this is very old, and deeply religious. In many ways it is breathtaking, yet at some level we all understand the terrorist. He or she is part of us and we of them.

Terrorists are murderers, that is clear. They do everything to destroy the ordered community. They do exactly what the scapegoats* did in all the myths. At the same time, where culture* and structures are fading away, chaos is rising and we need scapegoats* desperately. Without knowing it consciously, we are actively seeking them. We, the non-terrorists need and wish them.

Terrorists offer their blood to be sacrificed for peace. This longing for peace is our longing too. According to a long Irish tradition, they seek deification by offering themselves, so procuring peace for the world. In a very deep sense, they are doing our business.

It is an understandable, if hopeless, undertaking. It is hopeless because the scapegoat* mechanism does not work in our modern world. Terrorists are sliding into a model-obstacle* relationship. They fight the invincible model in order to take his place – trying to win over the model and rule like gods. But, like everybody else, they perish once they get caught up in a model-obstacle* relationship.

We are told that life is impossible if we don't distinguish between the good and the bad. For our culture* this is undoubtedly the case. Our culture* is built on this premise and would end up in chaos without it. Because we are becoming indifferent about the difference, culture* is disappearing.

Bringing back the difference, which was only possible for culture* by scapegoating*, is now no longer possible. In that sense, terrorism is the last card culture* has to play in trying to restore itself. Scapegoating* destroys life. In fact we are destroying life without knowing what we are doing. It is done to make life possible for ourselves and for those who belong to us. Scapegoating* is the kernel of hypocrisy. At the same time, however, it is impossible to condemn the scapegoaters without becoming scapegoaters ourselves.

Learning this with our heads, rationally, is one thing, but we can be sure that as long as we only know this with our heads scapegoating* will continue. Existentially we only know about scapegoating* when we ourselves are scapegoated. In these circumstances life can be very hard for us. The only way out is to follow Jesus, who prayed for forgiveness for his scapegoaters because they did not know what they were doing. Our own scapegoaters don't know either. When we find a way to know this with our being, we can find a way out of the tangle and we are free.

We can look at the scapegoat* mechanism from another side, with the eyes of those afraid of becoming scapegoats*. We are all extremely afraid of becoming a scapegoat*. The great anxiety, the fear circulating in our culture*, is precisely the fear of becoming a scapegoat*, a fear which lies deep in our hearts. However, even though it is in our hearts this does not necessarily mean that we ever see reality with the eyes of the scapegoat* . Instead we shy away from it. We dare not see with the eyes of the scapegoat*.

The eyes of the scapegoat* are those in the face of the defenceless. Emmanuel Levinas, the Jewish philosopher, writes about these people in his work. They are the eyes of Jesus, who understands us better than we understand ourselves. The eyes of the victim, of the scapegoat*, of the defenceless, see the destructive and incomprehensible madness of this world. When we finally are the victims, we no longer fight our opponents. We only ask for humanity, for love.

In fact, the victim who knows that the fighting makes no sense, who knows that all of the fighting is over, is finally free. He or she is like a dying person, who knows that all the striving in their life only destroyed their life. Because the scapegoat* is free, the eyes of the victim make us free when we are prepared to meet them. In meeting the eyes of the scapegoat*, we come into mimesis* with them and we are freed for a new life.

16. Feelings

It is very important to distinguish between feelings in our modern western sense and Jesus' feelings in the gospels. Our feelings are in our breast. They are our emotions. When Jesus has feelings, which come when he sees people who are in distress, his feelings are in his guts, in his bowels. Feelings in the gospels and throughout the whole bible are feelings provoked by relationships lived in external mediation*. These feelings actually give form to the relationship in freedom*.

In contrast, our feelings tie us into model-rival* and model-obstacle* relationships and make us unfree. Although we usually assume otherwise, our modern feelings, like everything else, do not arrive in our breast from nowhere. Our feelings belong to and arise out of the rivalry and mimesis* of our relationships. As such, they tell us about our relationships. If we are to understand them, we have to translate the feelings back into the relationship with the person or people who give us these feelings.

All of our feelings have to do with relationships. They are never autonomous, arising in us because of unchanging qualities. They are not innate or personal. In our feelings we experience in ourselves our rivalrous relationships with other people, with cultural realities and with the gods. Often these relationships involve temporal mimesis* and there is always some spatial mimesis*. Meeting a person, a group or a situation in the present incites the repetition of an old experience in the form of feelings.

Many of our feelings are cultural. All of our aesthetic feelings, such as beauty, have to do with ritual, with the driving out of the scapegoat*. Consciously, of course, this is very far away, which is why feelings can be seen as purely aesthetic, unlinked to ritual. Our awareness of watching scapegoating* and ritual is at its closest in comedy and tragedy. It remains true, however, for all the aesthetic feelings which come when we hear a poem, music or see a picture. In every case the aesthetic experience results in us driving something out and we feel good.

Many other feelings are cultural as well, though not so universal, like feelings aroused by national symbols or memories. It is not important to go into this in detail.

What is true for shared cultural feelings is also true for all personal feelings. Our personal feelings are always to do with relationships with people or with a certain person. They have always something to do with the mimesis* of desire and hence with the process of scapegoating* and being scapegoated, rivalry and model-obstacle*s.

All of our emotional feelings come out of and belong to relationships. Learning this is a long process. For example, excitement has to do with rivalry and scapegoating*, depression with model-obstacle* relationships as has the constant sense of failure. Being afraid is the fear of being scapegoated. These are only a few examples. We will look at some more examples later (see section 17). In fact the task of translating our feelings into relationships is a task for the whole of our lives. However, it is a journey which brings us happiness each day as we reveal more and more.

Although at first glance it may appear to be very strange, it is nevertheless true that freedom* and emotional feelings exclude each other. Of course, feelings of happiness and achievement are wonderful. But these good feelings are the feelings of the winners – those who are one-up in the rivalry – while negative and sad feelings are those of the losers. We can be sure that all our feelings of elation are paid for by others, however unpalatable the thought may be.

If this is true, how do we get rid of feelings? In fact we often don't actually want to get rid of them, even in cases where the feelings and emotions have become dangerous for us or for others. The power-game which lies behind the feelings is just too exciting. But assuming that we want to escape them, how do we get rid of them?

In feelings we are tangled up in relationships. Therefore if we want to escape from our emotional feelings and be delivered from our difficulties we have to enter other relationships and enter another world in which the relations which provoke our feelings have no power. When friends urge us to 'come back down to earth', they mean exactly the same thing. Relationships evoking feelings isolate us from all of our other relationships. With all of our fascination*, all other relationships eventually seem meaningless to us. To be free, we have to find a way back to them.

17. Some examples of feelings

Our lives are increasingly closed up in internal mediation*. Because of the loss of external mediation*, we are losing all of our real relationships with the reality beyond ourselves. This not only means that life becomes more complicated. It also means that our ability to see reality is more and more 'skewed'. Increasingly, our feelings come between us and the world we live in. Perhaps if we differentiate between some of the feelings we have, we can get a clearer insight into what is happening.

a. *Feeling very good (elation) – feeling low (depression)*. We feel great about ourselves, we are happy with ourselves when we are in the one-up position – when we win against our rivals. When we lose, we are depressed and feel hopeless. In many cases this is difficult for us to understand. Often, we don't recognise the power battles with other people with whom we feel a deep relationship. When we feel continually happy, we can't understand that the other person is unhappy. We simply can't believe it. In winning, we become blind to the defeat of the other and to his or her feelings of being rejected.

b. *Being happy – being unhappy*. In fact this is about the same thing. We are happy while we are winning or for as long as the outcome of the fight for power has not been decided. On the erotic level this might mean that we are happy for as long as the other is amorous. We are unhappy when we are losing or fear that we might soon lose. For as long as there is still tension, life is exciting and dangerous in a sort of beautiful sense. I might win. On the other hand I might lose and then in the end I am unhappy. If I lose, if I end up in a model-obstacle* relationship or if I am left by the other, then in fact I am alone, left alone in my unhappiness.

Of course there is another possibility of happiness. This is the quiet happiness – the contentment of knowing that I am in my place, where nobody is rivalling with me and where I am not rivalling. This happiness has nothing to do with emotional feeling. This happiness comes from external mediation*, when we are living in relationships which carry us. Increasingly, this happiness is disappearing.

c. *Jealousy*. We are jealous when we are afraid of losing the power-battle or when we have already lost it. We are jealous when some-body has something which we desire, but which we will never possess. Jealousy means that we are imprisoned by our rival. We are fascinated by our rival. If a man is jealous because other men are looking at his wife or lover he is imprisoned by them and not by her. This is true even if she encourages the other men to desire her. He is rivalling with them, event-ually even forgetting about her. It may be that she becomes very afraid because of his jealousy but the jealousy is still about them and not about her. Jealousy is always about the rival. Nevertheless, the object of the rivalry, in this case the woman, has well-founded fears. Jealousy is full of violence and violence can switch at any time from the opponent to the 'object' of the rivals' desires.

d. *Fascination**. Jealousy is one form of fascination*. Fascination* is often a marvellous feeling. We also know that it is a risky feel-ing, a risky experience. Eventually we can end up like quivering wrecks. We only recognise fascination* when it has become strong. Every relationship in internal mediation*, all model-rival* and model-obstacle* relationships, are fascinations. In everyday speech we reserve the word fascination* for very strong feelings in the field of erotic desire and aesthetics. If we talk in terms of structures however, all of our mimetic relationships are about fascination* as soon as our rivals have any power over us.

In fascination*, the other gains power over me, in me. Fascin-ation* is my internal fight against the other person in me who claims me totally, ultimately claiming every aspect of my being. The other might be a person, a group, an ideal or whatever. Ultimately, the fascination* is so powerful that the fight not to lose myself entirely becomes dominant. All other possibilities around me, all of my other relationships, disappear. As the fasci-nation* deepens, the feelings become ever more dominant and the powerfight encompasses ever more of me. The more the fasci-nation* deepens, the more it is revealed in its true character.

No matter how nice they are, our emotional feelings are always a form of slavery. When a fascination* passes a certain point, we see how serious this slavery is. Fascination* becomes obsession. For as long as we are fascinated and we still have the feeling that we will or can reach our goal it is a wonderful feeling. As soon as we lose, we are lost. All of the crimes of passion, the last desperate attempt to win, come out of this. Neurosis and psychosis also have the same root. Fascination* is the mark of illness in human relationships. As such it is neither an erotic nor an aesthetic reality. At the same time, as soon as there is fascination* between men and women about any object, eroticism is present in some form or other.

e. *Sadism and Masochism*. We all want to be gods. Furthermore we wish to prove that we are gods to all those in our power, all those who adore us and make us gods. It is also possible that we can find pleasure in continually losing. We too can enjoy adoring the god who defeats us. In losing and in accepting everything which is done to us, we prove to ourselves that our model, the object of our metaphysical desire, is in fact a real god, an invincible model.

This is nevertheless a double bind. If we ever did win, we would be gods ourselves. At one and the same time the winning is pointless because in winning we would show that our gods were in fact not gods and not what we thought them to be. When we are closed in a model-obstacle* relationship and we are losing, we choose to remain to our position. We force the other to be a sadist. He or she has to show that he is the almighty, above all the laws and morals – a god. If the power in the relationship turns around, which happens very frequently in many relationships, then I am the sadist and the other is the masochist. In the end, nobody wins and nothing is won. More clearly than ever, the plus and the minus, winning and losing, are the same.

f. *Anger and fear*. Fear is always the fear of losing. The fear can be so great as to be paralysing. I can't defend myself. The figure of the other is so powerful in me that he takes me over. I am no longer myself. In anger we defend ourselves against fear and against the other in us. In our anger we try to throw him out of us and be free of his power.

g. *Tears and laughter*. With both, we defend ourselves against the other within us. As long as we are laughing, the situation is not too dangerous. We can be a little violent also, trusting that we will win. We laugh and so we push others out. When we are crying, the situation is nearer to us and more dangerous. We try to get rid of the danger of being overwhelmed by the other, whoever or whatever the other may be.

h. *Enthusiasm*. Enthusiasm is a religious word. In enthusiasm we are actually possessed by a god, by gods. We are overpowered and we rejoice in it. Even if we are pushed away and ignored, we accept it. It is religious, so in enthusiasm we are always scapegoating* and have in fact succeeded in driving something or somebody out. Enthusiasm has always destroyed somebody or something and real human possibilities.

i. *Eroticism and sexuality*. For us, both eroticism and sexuality seem inseparable from feelings. We don't even know any more that sexuality is possible without feelings, in freedom*, and that it has a very important ritual meaning for our lives. Both eroticism and sexuality have now to do with rivalry and the powerfight. We give the other entrance into us and the possibility to win over us, or the possibility to lose. Alternatively, we get bored with the fight and decide that it is not so interesting after all. ('I am absolutely certain that I don't love her.') We leave one battlefield and move to another. We cannot imagine our lives nowadays without this excitement. The endless trail of stranded ships on the shoreline, stranded in life by these fights, remind us continually of how we get along with each other.

j. *Ideals and ultimate goals*. As soon as we have feelings about ideals and great goals we are building them up into model-obstacle*s. Instead of us being their masters, being free of them and even free for them, they have taken us over. In fact, when we have ideals and great goals we are trying to control the future. Because we are unable to do that, we become slaves of our models and they become obstacles. As a result they inspire great feelings.

Ultimately, there is only one way out of all the rivalrous feelings. It is the way of Jesus, the man who is outside of desire and hence outside the power game. He is beyond the world of feelings. He is always calling us. In meeting him, in following him, we are free of the feelings which destroy us.(see part 2)

A lot of us may find all of this very odd. Their relationship to Jesus is full of feelings. For most of us, believing has everything to do with feelings and very deep feelings at that. And despite this, it remains true that for as long as there are feelings in our relationship with Jesus, it is not faith*. We are in faith* when we are 'simply' in the world of Jesus, with our very being, following him because we know that he is the Way. This knowing is not intellectual but an existential knowing with the totality of our being – heart, body, brain. It is an all-pervasive knowledge that Jesus is the way, the truth and the life.[20] This knowledge sets us free, giving peace and delivering us from our feelings.

We can never forget the difference between our language about feelings and that of the gospels. Our feelings, in our breasts or our hearts, come from the mimesis* of desire. When Jesus has compassion, a verb is used implying that they come from his guts, from his bowels. These feelings are wholly other realities to our emotional feelings. In modern feelings the other occupies me, even if the feelings are beautiful. Gut feelings are a sign that we allow the other into our life. Through these feelings we recognise the other, seeing them defenceless and helpless.

When we follow Jesus, we are delivered from our feelings at last. For as long as we are enslaved by the mimesis* of desire, we are the slaves of our feelings. Following him, we are free. There is only joy in belonging to him.[21] There is only compassion in fellowship with him.

18. Relations and trust

Again, we have not become what we are through inherent characteristics. Everything we are, we have learnt in mimesis* with others. This is how we got our 'character' (which is the way in which we interact with the reality in which we live) and our 'personality' (which is the way we are perceived by others and, perhaps differently, by ourselves). We are given and become what we are and who we are. Others give it to us while we give to others. This process continues throughout our lives.

Our whole reality is mimesis*: Not only our heart or our thinking or our bodies but every possibility we have as human beings takes place in mimesis*. We are born into and live in mimesis*. It is our condition. As such mimesis* happens whether we think about it or not. Mimesis* happens first. Mostly we don't perceive it, let alone reflect on it. This means that there is knowledge in our beings which is neither conscious in our heart nor in our head. Ultimately, it is deeply rooted in us – in our feet. We find ourselves being brought somewhere by our feet even when our head and our heart are struggling against it or are unaware of it. We can rest assured that they know more than we know consciously. This does not mean that our feet are always doing good or taking us into freedom*. They can of course take us into the slavery of fascination*. However, if our feet bring us in the Way of Jesus, even if our head and our heart are shrinking away from it because of the consequences, we can trust them.

If mimesis* of desire does not stop and we remain in all of our mimetic relationships, life becomes permanent fighting as it has become for many people. It is a struggle not to drown in the power game and be totally destroyed.

Having grown up in the learning process in mimesis* with the old model, the model has to 'die' for us, so that we become free again. Culture* created the possibility of letting models die through 'rites of passage', the rites through which people came into a new stage of life with its new responsibilities and possibilities.

Confirmation, baptism, bar mitzvah, marriage, military service were, and to some extent still are, such rites. These old institutional possibilities are no longer solid foundations. One of the consequences is that we never really become grown-ups.

There is an escape from the eternal fight which is at the same time a way to be. Jesus says on several occasions: I am. He can say a sentence ending it with 'because I am'.[22] The fact that 'he is' explains, in a sense, everything. 'He is' because he is in mimesis* with the Father. Being in mimesis* with the Father, Jesus simply is. Because he is in mimesis* with the Father he is outside the mimesis* of desire when he meets other people. Jesus cannot lose the fact that he is. That he is, in his manner, means peace and means freedom*. Thus he is the Way to this freedom*.

We are free when we are in mimesis* with him, no longer doubting that we are. Then we are able to be outside the mimesis* of desire, outside the struggle. We are as simple as Jesus himself.

We exist in relationships. This means that we do not have 'individual' or 'personal' difficulties. In a sense we are always scapegoating* people when we make their difficulties 'personal' or 'theirs'. In so doing, everybody else escapes their responsibilities and their share in the difficulties. All the difficulties we find ourselves in, all the feelings and experiences we are struggling to overcome, are the others. In fact, they too have the difficulties with us, even though they deny it with a clear conscience. In their lives too, mimesis* precedes consciousness.

Because all our relationships are formed in mimetic patterns, we also shape the reality of other people. If we trust another person then he or she feels ground beneath his or her feet. It means that he or she can become trusting and so themselves trustworthy. If we fail to trust somebody, they are also in mimesis* with that lack of trust and will become exactly what we expect from him or her. The other acts untrustworthily and we feel vindicated. We tend not to be aware of the fact that we created the situation and actually desired it, for whatever reason. We reached our goal. By trusting we do not reach a 'goal' but we reach the other.

19. What is freedom?

Even though we use the word freedom* so often, we are very unclear as to what it means. What is freedom*? Let us begin by saying what we mean: Freedom* means to be out of the mimesis* of desire, out of model-rival* and model-obstacle* relationships. Unfreedom means to be in mimesis* of desire. The story of the Garden of Eden and the Fall from Paradise is the story of moving from the freedom* of not-desiring into the unfreedom of the mimesis* of desire.[23]

Culture* provided the possibility to live within a kind of freedom*. By its structures and laws, and through its prohibitions and rules, it made it possible for people to be themselves, not constantly at odds with everybody and everything. It was a restricted freedom* in that it was founded on the scapegoat* mechanism. We are free within culture* because the scapegoats* are carrying parts of us. They carrey those possibilities within ourselves with which we cannot cope, our violence and guilt. Their existence carried and carry our problems away for us. You found freedom* if you stuck to your place, took no more rights than you were given and fulfilled your duties. In accepting your human task you had the possibility to be yourself and to be at peace. As long as the hypocrisy was an overall cultural phenomenon and you were oblivious to it, it was objective hypocrisy. Cultural freedom* meant that you gave the others the same freedom* to live always provided that they were not the scapegoats*. Freedom* was possible if everyone stuck to their boundaries.

Structure* and law are fading away. Ironically, we usually assume that we are more free than ever just because of this disappearance. As long as we succeed in the endless fight for the position of top-dog, in which we participate even though we often don't acknowledge it, we can appear reasonably or even very happy with the situation. As soon as we end up one-down, whether personally, or as a group or as a nation, things deteriorate. We become unhappy and depressed, finding ourselves in a labyrinth without an escape. Our freedom* always depends on making others unfree.

Yet one freedom* remains: We can always choose differently. Mostly we don't choose for long, or at most we choose within the context of our daily lives being reasonably sure of what will happen next. Nevertheless the choice remains a possibility. We can choose to do our duty whatever the costs may be. We can choose to follow an ideal which we have had for a long time. In both cases an external mediation* has come into our lives. As long as we stay true to this choice we are not in rivalry with the people around us, or at the very least it is less direct. We are most probably in an oblique transcendence*. We may act foolishly but at least we choose and are free in our choosing.

The great problem with choices, even small choices, is that it always entails risk: We never know the consequences in advance. These are choices which have to do with the whole of our lives. We are free to make the choice and we have to take the risks. Only after the event will we know what happens to us because of that choice. This scenario makes us so afraid that we mostly think that we have no possibility to choose at all. Here we have revealed something of a paradox: we only choose because we trust and we trust because we choose.[24]

All this is true when we choose to follow Jesus in freedom*, to be in mimesis* with him and so to be in mimesis* of not-desiring, outside desire. Jesus says something about what will happen to us when we make that choice.[25] Nevertheless, at the moment of choice, we are in complete uncertainty about what will happen to us. One thing is sure: I will change and everything will change. How? In what ways?

We are free to choose who we follow. We are free at this moment to choose. Whether we are free and how far we are free after the choice, depends on the choice. This is not freedom* as it is always presented to us or as we usually see it in front of us. Modern freedom* means being able to do what we want when we want as we want. This is the freedom* of internal mediation* in which everybody makes their own laws. It is an illusion of freedom*. It is the freedom* of those who are one-up, the winners in the rivalry.

When Jesus stands before us he asks us, he invites us, to him.[26] It is not the kind of challenge which we normally think of. It is much more peaceful. He invites us to follow him and to be free – freed from the constraints of the mimesis* of desire. We can be free to be and free to give others the possibility of being themselves without fear of being recognised or of being unmasked. Finally we can be open, children of God.

PART TWO

The New World – The Kingdom

Deep within all of us there is a longing for peace. This is a deep wish founded on the age-old cultural memory which lives in us all and which has been known by all people in all times. Peace might mean sacrificial peace or else it is the longing for the Kingdom of God, a longing for the world or culture outside the mimesis of desire. For most of us it will be a mixture of the two.

The Kingdom is not a memory. It is the possibility of a new life which is given to us. The existence of this world is a revelation for us. In fact it is the true meaning of revelation: The possibility or indeed the reality of another life in which there is freedom* and peace. Love.

In our times, with structure* and transcendence* disappearing, the longing for peace is growing deeper. We are desperately seeking the possibility to live in peace and yet we destroy it ourselves over and over again. In fact, in this longing, we are travelling from the longing for sacrificial peace to a longing for the Kingdom, the new world. We are all on our way out of this world into the new world. Maybe we will always be on our way, travelling far but never leaving this world, looking at the new from afar. Yet, now and then, often without really noticing it, we might take steps into the Kingdom. Without us knowing exactly what is happening, the Kingdom is suddenly around us.

Following Jesus is the Way.[27] If it is given to us, we join in as a community. We will go and show the way to each other and to those around us.

'As it is, these remain: faith*, hope and love, the three of them; and the greatest of them is love.' (1Cor. 13,13)

20. The God of the scapegoats

The gods of religion* are the gods of the scapegoaters. They are the gods of all the 'good' people. They are our gods. These gods have all the same possibilities as us. They can be both nice and dreadful. They have our violent side – the side which we don't really want to know about. We can see these qualities when we look at our gods and their characteristics. Inasfar as we are afraid of them, we are afraid of ourselves. We are afraid of the devil, the scapegoat* who we ejected yet who is at the same time an object of worship, our god.

The God of the scapegoats* is completely different. The Hebrews began to discover him when they lived through the experience of being scapegoats*, surviving while the scapegoaters perished. It was the experience that there was indeed more to heaven and earth than religion* had dreamt about.

The God of the scapegoats* has 'the face of the victims' – the face which the philosopher Levinas describes in his work over and over again. He is not demanding, ferocious or subject to whim, neither is he a do-gooder. He is not like the gods of the scapegoaters. He only asks us to give ourselves to him and to experience, like the scapegoated, that we are living in abundance and freedom*, in a land of milk and honey. In that land we are living outside desire.

This God, who has no power at all, is the almighty liberator from the land of slavery. Through the fact that He has no power at all, we see that He is all-powerful, He gives everything. All the gods of religion*, the gods of power, reduce space by taking space for themselves. After the gods have taken their space, the people have to fit into the rest. The God of the scapegoats* gives space. After a while the Hebrews or Israelites came to the conclusion that everything, all space, belongs to Him. He is the God of the whole earth. Everybody who belongs to Him also inherits all of the space, everything.[28] We can only find this God if we are together with the weak, the poor, the dispossessed, the victims of culture*. In other words, if we are with the scapegoats*. We can find Him if we open our hearts to them, recognising our human situation and theirs and knowing that there is only life for us if and when we are together with them.

The words of Exodus 20:12 say this to us, the words which introduce the Ten Commandments: I liberated you from the bonds of slavery in Egypt and led you through the desert. I gave you food and water, protecting you from your enemies. I was your guide and safety for forty years. In the end, I brought you to the land of milk and honey. I gave you everything. All you had to do was to follow me. Therefore you no longer need to do what all the other peoples tend to do – all the things mentioned in the Ten Commandments. In fact, for as long as you know me and live in my abundance, you will not forget about all these things.

After this introduction, the Ten Commandments follow. They remind us of all the things we did before we knew Him, things which destroyed us. For the Israelites, the journey to this discovery was a very long one. They had some ideas from the very beginning, intuitions, which they did not forget. They began to write down their history in a new way. They no longer wrote the story as that of the scapegoaters but rather as the history of the scapegoats*. They understood that all scapegoats* were as innocent as they were. In exactly the same way, our scapegoats* are as innocent as we are. In a process over many centuries, they learnt more about this strange God, whose strength is built on weakness.

We have to go the same way as they did if we want to meet Him, to follow Him, to be in mimesis* with Him and hence become free. Once more and at last we become made in His image. Once more we recognise ourselves and Him in the servant of Yahweh.[29]

21. The man Jesus

Jesus is the man outside desire. He is in mimesis* outside desire, in mimesis* with God and hence clearly in external mediation*. He is exactly the same as us except that he is without desire or, as the letter to the Hebrews puts it, without sin.[30]

The Gospel shows that it is this fact which marks him out more than anything else: The fact that he does not desire. The story of the temptations in the wilderness brings this out.[31] The story is in fact a repetition of the temptation in the Garden of Eden, except that the outcome is reversed. Satan is expelled. If we can understand this, the meaning of the gospel becomes clear.

Jesus is the goal and the end of the journey which the Israelites had been on since their ancestors fled from Egypt. The authors of the gospels show us this connection by underlining it time and time again. They use phrases from the Old Testament far more often than we are aware. The truth which the Old Testament is seeking after, and often showing, finds its embodiment in Jesus. He is the Word of God.[32]

At the same time both Jews and non-Jews were extremely puzzled. How could it be that Jesus was who he was? And why was it just him? We will never know why and nevertheless we do know that he is He. The first community tried to make the story comprehensible by using and translating myths, showing that the scapegoat* is not the guilty one but rather the innocent one in the midst of the scapegoaters. They did this by building up the story of his life. More profoundly, they took steps into the dark, hoping to find light. This is exactly the Way which we have to go.

Jesus is outside desire. John says in his Gospel that Jesus does what he sees the Father doing, speaking the words which the Father speaks to him.[33] In mimesis* with God, Jesus finds that he is himself. He is the image of God, being completely in mimesis* with God. Thus he shows God to us.[34] The only real knowledge we have of God we get by looking at him and hearing him.[35] In the Old Testament we read about the age-long spiritual fight between the gods of the peoples – the devil-gods – and the God of the scapegoats*. In the gospels everything becomes clear at last.

Because he is outside desire, Jesus knows and sees. He has the freedom* to see everything and as a result he knows. He knows the Way to be free, to be with the father, and at the same time he knows which ways lead away from him and to destruction.[36] Jesus knows about the rivalrous causes of mental and physical illnesses. He heals the sick just by being with them. Jesus asks them to follow him and to be free of rivalry and all of its consequences.

The Hebrews came to understand that Yahweh gave them freedom* when they were in slavery, the slavery of culture*. In finding Him, they found that they lived in abundance. In the same way, Jesus gives everybody who follows him new life, freed from the straightjacket of the law. What this new life means is described in the Sermon on the Mount. It is not a law; it is a promise (see section 23).

All the statements which we find so contradictory when the Old Testament talks of Yahweh, we find resolved in Jesus. He is powerless and as a result he is the almighty. On the cross, he disarms all the powers of this world because he exposes the secret of their power, the secret of the scapegoat* mechanism.[37] He asks for forgiveness for us the scapegoaters. Once we understand that he is asking forgiveness for us, he sets us free. Weakness becomes strength, poverty becomes wealth, low becomes high and so on. In the gospels, the whole world is turned upside down.

On the cross, Jesus shows us ultimate reality. Being powerless, the fulfilment of life begins. Once we are really powerless, we can no longer rival with anybody else. All of our rivalry, all of our powergames slip away from us and we find the freedom* of Christ, having everything in nothing. The deaths of Don Quixote and of Julien Sorel, the hero of Stendhal's novel 'The Red and the Black', are hinting at this reality. They learn that all rivalry is self-destructive, and Julien even wishes to die with this knowledge rather than go back into the rivalling world. We know something of this. What little we know of it, we know through looking at Jesus.

This reality of Jesus outside desire, is the only true reality. He is always dying as long as we are scapegoating* others or ourselves. If we look at him, he sends us on the Way of life with his spirit – sending us to the others. The foundation and explanation of everything he says and does is the fact that he truly is. When we are together with him, we become free – human, as he is.

This is how Jesus can say about himself 'I am', and everything he says and does he says and does 'because I am'. He is the only human being who truly is. In belonging to him, we really are.

22. Faith

Faith* means following Jesus, going the Way. This does not mean trying to be the same as him. Pietists strove after the goal of being as good, as nice, as superhuman as the Jesus of their fantasies. We can never reach such a goal, although this is not the real reason why we shouldn't try. Our task is to become ourselves, in the freedom* of Jesus, not to become a bad copy of him.

Following Jesus means to be in mimesis* with him as the man outside desire. From the outset, it is external mediation* because Jesus does not live physically in our world. Furthermore it is a vertical transcendence* as well. Because we are together with the man outside desire, we cannot rival with him and make the transcendence* oblique. Being in mimesis* with Jesus means that all of the possibilities of life and the world are opened up for us. We are free.[38]

One of the great difficulties for us living in our culture* is to understand the seeming contradiction that Jesus is both an external mediator and yet he is amongst us, in our midst whenever two or three are gathered in his name.[39] 'Being together in his name' means that we recognise him in each other. We are in mimesis* with him and hence outside desire. When we are following him together, each of us is Jesus for the others, because we no longer rival with one another, trying to be important.

In terms of our diagrams, being with Jesus means that we do not build up, do not rival. Rather, we remain as we are; we become a dot. Without him, we rival with one another, becoming bigger and bigger or sinking deeper and deeper into a pit as we try to match and overpower our rival. When we meet Jesus, we no longer need to build up. We become dots and now, for the first time, we can go together with him through the eye of a needle.

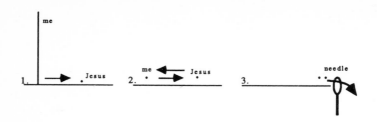

Following Jesus – who is the image of God – means that we too become the image of God.[40] This is the image in which Jewish thinking said we were created and which we lost as a result of desiring.[41]

Faith* also has to do with the Holy Spirit. We can meet Jesus without recognising who he is. He is in fact a very curious, maybe even special, person. He is very difficult for us to cope with. So many people have met him, time and time again, and did so without recognising him. Recognising him is not within our power; it is given to us. It is the Holy Spirit who works through the people around us and who opens our eyes when Jesus looks into them. The Spirit gives us the relationship, gives us faith* and makes us free.

Can we say anything more about choosing? Choosing means looking at the man Jesus and letting him be a reality. We choose by doing – by doing his work. We choose with our hands, our feet and our eyes. This is far more than choosing with our minds or our feelings. Our bodies and our feet know many things which our minds and feelings will never know, or which they know only dimly and in retrospect.

Paul always wanted to do everything in the service of Jesus. As a result he was always very disappointed about any mental or physical difficulties which hindered him. He prayed that he might be free of them, so that he could do more. Then he got the message that in his present state he was exactly right. In his weakness he was the right man. In praying he got the right answer, 'My grace is enough for you; my power is at its best in weakness.' (2 Cor 12, 9). This is once again the reality of the cross. It is exactly when we choose in weakness, with empty hands, that we are given the Way to go.

23. The Sermon on the Mount and the parables

Jesus brings a new world, a world which according to the Old Testament has been lost. This new world is not 'of this world'. Every world has its own language. The language of an adult is not the same as that of a child, the language of a man is still not entirely that of a woman. All are languages of culture*.

Jesus cannot use the language of this culture*. Were he to do so, he would be 'back to normal', back into this world. To make himself clear, Jesus turns everything upside down – low becomes high, poverty becomes wealth, strong becomes weak and vice versa, as success becomes failure and might is powerlessness.

In this gospel world, where our world is turned around 180 degrees, there is no longer a power struggle. The very fact that there is no power struggle turns everything on its head. As a result, Jesus cannot use our language. Our very language is in itself a power-struggle, seeking to objectivate everybody and everything. This process of making everything an object is accelerating all the time in modern times.

Jesus tells stories, the parables. Parables have an endless variety of meanings and cannot be pinned down once and for all. They have as many open-endings as life itself, just as Jesus has. These parables are very simple stories about simple life. They are just about facts. These facts are not the same as the so-called facts of our personal myths and culture*'s myths. They are about the reality – the facts – of life. As a result these parables abolish our world and our assumptions. They do away with our world by showing us ultimate reality, though not by fighting against reality, trying to impose our version, as we always do. Rather, they show the reality in such a manner, that it is impossible to fight against it. Our only choice in the face of these parables is to agree or to turn away.

Jesus tells us about how life in the Kingdom is, for example in the Sermon on the Mount.[42] This so-called sermon is actually neither a sermon nor a law. In this talk, Jesus describes and promises to us how life will be, when we hear him. In fact he describes the future of those who follow him.

The Sermon on the Mount and the parables are not defensive; they are open and vulnerable. This is true of everything Jesus says. Those who know him, take the words in the literal sense. They do not translate them into the world of religion* and culture* or make images of them. It is the truth for them who know him. They are the truth, but only when we let the words speak to us exactly as they are written down. Otherwise they lose their meaning and are used against Jesus – against the faith*.

We often use the gospels as a weapon against others, rather than to show ourselves who we are. We end up seeking to show others that they are wrong, or that they don't live up to what Jesus is saying. In so doing we make a weapon to destroy others out of the words of life – the gospels. The beam is in our eye at the very moment we do so, because we see the splinter in the eye of our brother.[43] The more pious and sophisticated we are, the greater is the risk that we use the gospel against our neighbours and use the gospel against itself. To be clever and learned is dangerous.[44] Most of us in western Europe today qualify!

There are a number of ongoing discussions in the gospels. For most of us they are very difficult passages. We see in them the discussions we have ourselves and we react to them in the same way. In the end, we simply shrug our shoulders, with the non-commital 'he might be right', or 'Of course he is right, but it doesn't really matter to me'. This is mostly because we like to overlook the fact that, at best, we are exactly the same as the pharisees. Often we assume that following Jesus is about being good people and that we are already good people because we are christians.

There are images in the gospels as well. The same thing happens to them as happens in the parables. Everything is turned upside down. One of the best known images is that of the lamb, the helpless sacrifice which conquers the world by suffering and shows us who we are.[45]

All of us are permanently rivalling, building ourselves up, trying to become bigger and bigger and as a result become more important. Jesus does not build up. He does not try to become big by rivalling and struggling. He just stays with himself, as he is, as a dot in our diagram. This unique person (not the most important which would be rivalry once more) is invisible in the power game. By coming into mimesis* with him, both together and alone, reading the bible, speaking to him and to the Father in prayer, we will come to resemble him step by step. In so doing, our deepest wishes will be fulfilled. Simultaneously, it goes against all of our wishes. We become nonentities in the eyes of the world, a dot.

24. Love

So many very different relationships are described as love that it might be useful to distinguish between them.

1. *Love in structure**. Structure* means that everybody has their own place with their own duties and rights. The most important point to note in this case is that everybody is different. Because we are different, we respect each other and let everybody else have their own place. We do not rival.

This is the basis of marriage in culture*. Husband and wife had their own territory. Everything was clearly defined. Very often they did not even choose each other; their families matched them. As a result even the choice was not a matter for rivalry between the partners. They 'simply' could accept and love, each other. Because everyone lived in structure*, everybody else's husband or wife were also clearly different. The same was true for friendships. Each friend had his or her own place and their own character. Each friend was different, and there was no rivalry.

In structure* I can have love for a larger group as well: for my community, my church, my country. I belong to it and I am different, with my own responsibilities and rights.

2. *Love when structures are disappearing*. Differences disappear with the disappearance of structure*. Rivalry increases. We rival with one another over partners. When we get a partner, we rival each other about them or for new partners. Whenever there is equilibrium in the power game, life is exciting and we feel very happy, although there is always an underlying anxiety because we are never sure what will happen tomorrow. Tomorrow we might be the scapegoat*, the loser.

If rivalry comes out into the open, life is even more exciting but the fear grows equally. The threat of violence is always close. Now and then it is difficult to distinguish acts of love from acts of violence. Fascination* grows with the rivalry.

Another possibility is that the partners become model-obstacle*s for one another, one having the role of sadist, the other being the masochist, although often the roles switch quickly to and fro between the partners . In such relationships, deep attachment, fascination*, and deep unhappiness often go together. Considerable violence can lie deeply hidden for a long time, but every now and again it can erupt, often totally unexpectedly. When it does it may destroy everything, including the life of one, or even both, of the partners.

The consequences of the disappearance of structure* are very important for relationships with larger communities. Increasingly we all try to win power over the community, or the church or the party. In extreme cases the community becomes our model-obstacle*. When this happens, we blow up its importance out of all proportion and sacrifice ourselves to it. Whether we do it in secret or in the open, we become fanatics. This is very often the case in Northern Ireland. The opposite can also happen when we don't have any power within our community, nor can we get it. For that reason, without being conscious of it, we effectively disappear, becoming sleeping members of our community.

3. *Love outside desire.* Outside desire there is no rivalry, no measurement against anybody else. The other can be who he or she is and we can love them as such. Likewise, we can be as we are. We are like the angels in heaven, angels being without desire.[46] This in fact is the only difference between them and us. In the love of Jesus we find the possibility of knowing ourselves, and knowing each other.

Love in structure* and in disappearing structures is called 'eros' in the New Testament. Eros is not bad as such. It is the attachment we have for one another in culture*, and it is one of the wonderful realities of life, although, as differences wane, it is being taken away from us more and more. Eros becomes another endless rivalry. Love outside desire is called 'agape' in the New Testament.

Love is always given, and we can never treat it as our tool, our weapon. People who threaten to withdraw their love do not know what love is. Love is given more easily to people living in structures than to people living in times when structures disappear, because they were not living in permanent rivalry. Without structures, love – eros – is like walking a tight-rope; you might succeed in balancing, but falling off is possible at any moment. Agape always comes from another world, from the world outside of desire. It is a gift transforming life, even if only for a moment. Yet at the same time it is a gift whose consequences we will maybe never entirely know. The gift changes our life.

25. The Law

Throughout the history of all culture*, the task of the law has been to prevent desiring. Desiring means rivalry, and eventually leads to chaos and the destruction of culture*. As a result, desiring was forbidden. The Ten Commandments reflect this. It is forbidden to desire to manipulate God and to have power over Him. Similarly, desiring to destroy structures, to have everything, is also forbidden.

In the Kingdom, there is no desire. You already have everything – much more than you could ever imagine. This message is already the core of the Ten Commandments. I, your God, delivered you out of the land of Egypt. I gave you and will give you everything. Because you know that I give and will give you everything you will not do all the things you would do if you did not know me, which you would do even though they are forbidden. You will not, you need not, desire.

Christ says the same: if you follow me I will give you everything you need; milk and honey, abundance. You will live out of the gifts which come to you from being together with me. All of this will be given, with persecutions too. The old Hebrews knew about this and we will know too if we follow Jesus.

If we follow Christ, if we are in mimesis* with him, we receive his freedom* and so know about his love for us and for our neighbour. Being in mimesis* with him, we can love our neighbours as we love ourselves and love God. Following Christ, we fulfil his 'completion of the law'.[47]

Following Jesus, being in mimesis* with him, means being free, because freedom* is being outside the mimesis* of desire. Being free has the direct consequence that we live in abundance. At last we can see just how many possibilities there are around us, the things that are invisible to us for as long as we are 'blinded' by our rivalries. While we are rivalling, we can only see our rivals and the object of our desire. Until now we were in a power-game with the others. We were not really seen as we are, but only in our role as (possible) rivals in the power game. In mimesis* with Jesus we are seen clearly as we are and we see the others and the world around us. At last we love each other as ourselves. The consequence is abundance.

And there will be persecutions.[48] Religion* is not dead. The scapegoat* system of religion* and culture* continues to seek the abnormal and turn them into scapegoats. The follower of Jesus is abnormal for culture*, and as a result is scapegoated, declared guilty indeed declared to be the only truly guilty one. Here again, religion* ends in a curious contradiction. The really innocent one is declared to be the only truly guilty one because he is outside desire. From the point of view of culture*, the innocent one is rightly declared guilty. The really innocent one exposes the hypocrisy of culture*. What is done to Jesus will be repeated to his followers, to those belonging to him. Were Jesus to return, he would be persecuted again, persecuted by the Grand Inquisitor in the *Brothers Karamazov* or by us. The Church always persecuted those who tried to follow Jesus. And nevertheless there is abundance.

Living in mimesis* outside desire means that nobody is an opponent any longer. Because violence has disappeared, there are no longer any scapegoats, but there are also no more opponents. Opponents only exist for as long as we are rivalling or when they are our obstacles. Being in mimesis* outside desire, means that this whole world vanishes. We are free and recognise our brothers and sisters. Everybody is our brother and sister, without exception. We belong to everyone, but first of all to the groups mentioned in Matthew 25. They carry the mark of Jesus on their faces, and when we forget them, we forget him. But if we only go to them to become their 'helpers' then we forget him as well.[49] Paul's deepest wish was to go to Rome and tell his story to the Emperor. In fact Jesus himself sent him.[50]

What it means in concrete terms to live as the people belonging to Jesus may well be an open question. We can only find the answer to it by going together. There are clues in the New Testament, and we have the wisdom collected by those who followed Jesus through the Ages. We also know that many ways are dead-ends. Ultimately, we must choose and go, both the old ways and on a new Way. The most important point is the choice, a choice made today and every day. We have the freedom* to choose. Not choosing is to choose for culture*, religion* and violence.

Paul's thinking on the law, especially at the beginning of the letter to the Romans reflects the complexity of its position. The law is good and sacred, because only in obedience to the law are we free from desire, free of slavery. At the same time, it is not possible to obey the law. As soon as we try, it becomes a model-obstacle* which destroys us. As a result the law is death. Jesus, by doing what he sees the father doing, being in mimesis* with God and hence outside of desire, obeys the law. He is outside of its realm. He abolishes the law in such a way that when we are in mimesis* with him – following him – we don't have to think about the law at all. We are beyond the scope of the law. As long as we are following him, and only then, the law is about nothing.

The exhortations which Paul gives the receivers of his letters often become reminders in their final parts: If we are these people, we belong to Jesus and are together in his name.

26. The world of culture
and the world of the gospel

To make things clearer, we drew a model, which showed us the differences between culture* and the gospel. We put things which belong to the world of religion* opposite things which belong to the world of faith*

*Culture**	*Gospel*
mimesis* of desire.	mimesis* outside desire.
we divide between good and bad.	we know that such division is hypocritical.
rivalry, we strive constantly.	no rivalry, we simply live.
scapegoating.	no scapegoating.
unfreedom.	freedom*.
cause leads to certain effect.	the unexpected.
the powerful and the rich are important.	the powerless and the poor are important.
hardships, ineed everything, are measured as gains and losses.	we are 'lilies of the field' without cares.
we exclude, driving out what we don't want.	we include and meet .
culture* and counter-culture*.	contrast-culture*, the Kingdom.
Everybody and everything are objects and a matter of 'objective' knowledge.	Everybody and everything is in the meeting or the relationship and changes in them.
Models show how 'things' are. Models freeze reality.	Models show what is happening between people and between people and their world.

We could certainly continue in this manner. Everybody could draw his or her own left and right world and it might be useful to do so. Each person has to go through their own wilderness of language to find clearings, to find spaces.

By putting the world of culture* and the world of the gospel opposite one another, we could give the impression that the journey with Jesus is a simple or mechanical movement from the left to the right world. The reality is more complex. As long as we are in this world, in this culture*, we are in mimesis* with it. At the same time, the reality of Jesus may well become stronger in our lives. We might even know that we can never fully lose sight of his reality because he knows us. In that sense we belong to the Kingdom. While we are in culture*, we never forget our meeting with Jesus. We know this with our being, with all of our existence as such. We move around in this world, carrying this other reality with us, our mimesis* always preceding consciousness and thinking. We can draw another model:

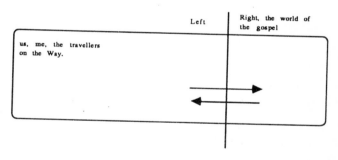

In effect, we are citizens of two worlds. We belong to the left hand world, the world of culture* and religion*. We also belong to the right hand world, knowing about it with the totality of our being. Very often we are living completely in the world of culture*, although we can never forget about the world of the gospel which now and then draws us into its reality. The way we experience this may be like the ancient procession in Echternach in Luxembourg where we move three steps forward and then two steps back. Sometimes it might be the opposite; going three steps back for every two steps forward. Nevertheless, the new Jerusalem is always before our eyes, ultimately growing closer.[51]

How do these two worlds inter-relate? What is the influence of the world of the gospel on that of culture*? We are moving with our lives or parts of our lives from the left to the right and back again. Anytime we are in the world of the gospels, in any manner whatsoever, our life in culture*, is changing. The rivalries in which we found ourselves are 'cut off' by the spatial mimesis* we find in freedom*. Of course we come into new ones or, in temporal mimesis*, we go back into the old ones. But first of all our old patterns are cut off. The whole of our life – and so our relations with everybody in it – is changed.

How is all of this possible? In the left world we are in the world of the mimesis* of desire, the world of rivalry. Everything we do is predictable following temporal mimesis* or, if we know more, it is understandable. Our lives go on in this way, until death. At death, we might finally succeed in seeing ourselves as we really are, perhaps for the first time. Then we succeed as Don Quixote and Julien Sorel succeeded.

When we come into the world of the gospel, the slavery to this chain of cause and effect is broken. We are free, which means that we are free of the cause and effect chain of rivalry and we do something different which by definition will be something unexpected. To do the unexpected means to break the chain of cause and effect . We can do the unexpected because, being free of the mimesis* of desire, we at last see the world and all of its possibilities. In freedom*, we can make new choices each time, very often without thinking about them. In our freedom* we are already choosing. After this experience, the world of culture* becomes reality again, but our world has changed. We return once more to the religious system but it has lost some of its enslaving possibilities. Through our lives, this is a learning-process with our very being. A model might look like this:

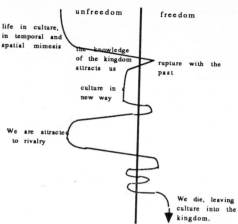

Every time we experience freedom*, the cause and effect chain is broken and it loses a little bit of its strength. Freedom* grows.

This all has to do with wisdom. We will never get out of mimetic circles of rivalry and out of model-obstacle* relationships by trying harder, by fighting to escape. By trying harder we only get more deeply involved. Again, the plus and the minus are the same. We seldom find this wisdom on our own, in isolation. We need each other to find a way to freedom*.

27. Language

Real change means that the whole of our life changes. When we step out of one culture* into another, every aspect of the culture* changes. When we move from the world of culture* into the world of the gospel, where everything is turned upside down, this is true to a breathtaking extent.

The change also applies to the language we use. Our language belongs to culture*, to religion*. It is the language of the scapegoating system, of the world of cause and effect where the scapegoat* is driven out. As time passes our language is becoming more and more technical, even when we are talking about human beings. Humanity itself is disappearing in our language as people become objects for study and nature has become an object to exploit. The humans around us are becoming objects for our manipulation. Our bodies are becoming the object of manipulation by the medical sciences. Our minds are open prey for the media – their very lifeblood – while death has become the last and greatest model-obstacle* of our time.

Of course we could easily extend this list, but it is unnecessary. Everything that is happening around us and in us today is the final consequence of our culture* in which language also has a major role. With our language we drive out all of human reality.

When we wander from the world of culture* into the world of the gospel we need another language. This language cannot scapegoat* anybody or anything, as scapegoating comes out of the world of cause and effect. The language of the gospel enables us to speak about the whole of reality, unlike cultural language which only speaks about the parts of reality which fit into culture* and only in the manner in which they fit into culture*.

The authors of the bible had to cope with this problem, as did Jesus. He tells parables and describes the new life. He shows the new life by doing, fusing word and action. He uses the language of children and of simple people. For the sophisticated, imbued in culture*, his language is mostly too difficult.

As always, the only possibility we have is to follow him. In fact this is very hard. We have to be aware of everything we say and do. It is a hard task, one of constant learning, requiring a lot of practice and where we will rely very much on help from one another. One very good and helpful way, if not a necessary one, is by reading and reflecting on the gospels and the bible as a whole. By so doing we come into mimesis* with the authors of the bible who tried so desperately to find the right sentences and the best words. Being in this mimesis*, the language of the bible becomes ours, as do the stories and the interpretation of reality which is given in the bible.

There is a great risk that we will repeatedly re-translate the 'rightish' language of the bible into the 'leftish' language of culture*. In fact we will do it constantly, because we don't understand or we don't want to understand what exactly we are doing.

If the narrative of the gospel and the bible does not become the basis of our own story and how we tell it, or, to put it another way, if the narrative of the gospel and the bible does not become the reality in which the story of our own lives move, the Way might be very hard.

The translation of the bible is one important area where we must be careful. A worthwhile translation renders the original text most truly when it remains in the world of the original text, when the language which tells about the words and actions of the God of the scapegoats is preserved. There is a great risk in modern translations that we destroy the language of the God of the scapegoats, by turning it into the language of culture* and religion* through trying to make sure that everything is said in a modern way. This doesn't mean, however, that we have to stick to a particular translation.

28. Two worlds: Some practical consequences

It might be useful to give some examples of the differences in meeting each other in the world of culture* (on the left) and the world of the gospel (on the right). In the left world, life is always about not losing, and if possible winning, even if this is hidden in very ingenious ways. We might even explain everything to ourselves and others in such a way that everybody agrees. Yet however beautifully hidden it is, our explanation is always about power and violence.

I do not really listen. I try to win my point, to convince the other, especially when they tell me that I am or was wrong. I rival with my words.	I listen to the other with the whole of my being. I bear it when they say things that hurt me. One way or another what they say is true.
I am convinced that the other is my guilty, and I search them out.	I seek my own responsibility, own guilt.
I divide between 'us' and 'them' where we are the goodies and they are the baddies.	I use the word 'I', taking responsibility for everything I say and do.
I use the possessive pronoun to exclude others, mine, yours, ours.	I only use them where they include the others.
I ask questions in order to make the the other unsure and thereby I hope to win.	If I put a question, I explain to other why I do so. I tell what I know, so making myself vulnerable.
I 'mind-read', not truly being with the other but with my own assumptions about them, using my assumptions against them.	I listen carefully to the other. I ask when I am unsure or am making assumptions.

When the other is embarrassed, I take advantage of it.

If they are embarrassed, I respect it. If possible I try to find out from them what the problem is, so that they are not embarrassed any more.

I evade the other's eyes, or I fight with my eyes, trying to discover weaknesses and win.

I look in the eyes of the other showing myself in my weakness. Looking into the eyes of Jesus I look at him or her.

I don't have time. I am too busy with things which are more important for me.

I am open to the other. I know that most of the things I am so busy with are in fact not important at all.

I speak about others who are not present, either scapegoating them, or using them in a power-game.

I never do this.

I deny the feelings and impressions others have and tell me about. I know better than they do.

I hear the other telling about their feelings and impressions and know that they are not matters for discussion.

I assume that you are happy to do a task without asking.

I always ask whether you would like to do it or not.

When you come to our group it is up to you to find a place in it.

When you come to us, we open up a place for you.

I use words such as 'simply', 'just', 'of course', 'honestly' 'common', 'as a matter of fact', the so hiding the reality.

I hear myself using these words and try and find out what I am hiding , even if I have to ask the other for help.

I use sectarian language, of the church, of a certain class, of science, translating humanity into ideology and simultaneously make the other unsure and uneasy.	I use common words, the simple words of the gospel, so making relationships possible.
I moralise, telling the other that they are wrong or that what they did was wrong. I gossip.	I recognise that as soon as I moralise and gossip I am speaking about myself (the beam and the splinter).
I use the Ten Commandments and the Sermon on the Mount against others, to judge them.	The Commandments and the Sermon on the Mount are the possibility for us to work out whether we are moving on the Way or moving away from freedom*.
I use the words 'ought', 'should', 'must', against others to force them to do things I use consider to be 'good'.	In freedom* we forget 'ought', 'should' and 'must'. We ask ourselves why we want to them.
I concede to the other, then add 'but', thus annihilating the concession.	We use only 'and', not denying our concession.
I 'simply' don't like someone and in so doing, scapegoat* them.	When I don't like somebody I seek the realities in myself which I see in the other and thus find a way to him or her and to myself.
I ask 'why?', knowing that there is no answer, so scapegoating the other. With 'why?' questions we imprison the other in the past.	I know that it is not about 'why?' but about 'what?' What will we do now, following Christ?

I become excited and try to convince the other to be like me.

I remain quiet, in freedom*, and try to 'be' rather than win.

I find excuses when things between us go wrong. 'I only tried to help.' 'I meant so well.' Thus we blame and scapegoat* the other.

I try and find out what I am doing wrong when the other did not respond as I hoped or wished.

When we are trying to find ways, I reject all others' plans thus closing doors on others, blocking creativity and keeping power.

I am always open to the reality that there are wholly other possibilities than I ever thought of.

I try to convince by making my statements stronger, 'In the name of God' and so on. When we do this we are scapegoating. Swearing is scapegoating.

I always use simple words, even when the situation is very complicated or distressing for me.

I manipulate the outcome, of course with the best of intentions. When I fail I become angry, and blame the other, saying 'I meant so well.'

I speak as openly as possible with the other and am happy with their choice when it is made in freedom*, even when I disagree with it.

I am 'concerned'. I worry about the other. In fact I am putting myself in the one-up position in relation to them.

I have compassion, suffering with them. Their suffering is my suffering. Together we find a way out and go together.

I have patients, clients, cases.

I am together with other people, trying to find a way for both of us.

29. The new world

We know a great deal about culture* and religion* and about the world which was built by them. Nevertheless, we always missed the most important thing there was to know about it, both as a culture* and personally; that culture* is founded on violence and objective hypocrisy. Anyhow, we do know a great deal, now more than ever.

We know very little about the new world. We see glimpses of it in the gospels, in the words and actions of Jesus and in the opening chapters of Acts. Every now and again we are presented with an open window and we see a little bit of it.

The mimesis* of desire is over and we are free. What this means for us is very difficult to imagine. Jesus says that in heaven we will not marry. We are together like the angels.[52] We are like angels in the sense that angels are outside the mimesis* of desire. As a result, we no longer need to possess, and we no longer need to be protected against our desires. Therefore we will not marry. This is only one example and it is a negative one in the sense that something which we take for granted now will no longer be. We do not know what it will be like as angels in heaven, not being married, nor even needing, or wanting, to be. We can only have our dreams.

We know that the new world is a world without time or with another time. Time and space as we know them belong to culture*. When the bible speaks of the new world it talks of eternity but again we do not know what that means. We can have our fantasies.

John has his dream in the Book of Revelation, a dream about the new Jerusalem coming from heaven. This is the new world which is a gift to us.[53] It is indeed a very precious dream, saying in its heart that the new world is more wonderful than any imagination or dream. This echoes Paul.[54] We all have our dreams, and it does not matter even if they are silly dreams as long as they are surrounded by the words of Paul.

The new world is a dream and it is also certainly a reality. In faith*, belonging to Jesus, and in mimesis* with him, we are sure of that. 'Now faith* is the substance of things hoped for, the evidence of things not seen.'[55] This beautiful sentence indicates a wonderful reality.

The new world is an invitation. It is certainly not the same as Utopia, a cultural dream for which we have to strive. It is the invitation of and into freedom*. Only when we are given freedom*, can we make the step which sets our lives free. We overcome our fears, which are very understandable, each time we take the step, take the risk. We are like the Israelites entering the promised land and having to conquer it over and over again by leaving our fears behind us. Everything conquered in this manner is given.

30. The world of the gospel: Contrast culture

The new world is not simply the reverse of the old. We will never find the Way into the new world by fighting against the old world and its mechanisms. In the eternal power battle, which is taught in the internal mediation* of our present day culture*, both sides are mirrors of each other . We can only remember that plus and minus are the same. When we fight against this world we can only get what we don't want, what we want to avoid. Fighting for peace always means more violence. To be against scapegoating means to be scapegoating others. The way into the new world can never be that of counter- or contra-culture*, a culture* which strives to overpower culture* as it exists.

Following Jesus we seek the culture* outside the mimesis* of desire. This is the Kingdom of God, the culture* in which we know each other and ourselves as we are, the world in which all hypocrisy, all violence and all rivalry has been done away with. It is the world in which our view of the other is not distorted by desire and rivalry. In the Kingdom, in this contrasting culture*, everything is turned around as it is in the gospels. The scapegoat* which is driven out in culture* is the centre of contrast-culture*, the culture* of the gospels. He is the only real human, who did not drive out his violence. Instead he carries the violence of all the others on himself.[56]

The weak, the helpless, the hopeless are in the midst of the Kingdom. They are the hope and the bridge for the rest of us who are still in power and are striving for it. They may still be striving as hard as they can. We, when we look at them in the freedom* of Christ, can make them free. Contrast culture*, the Way of the Kingdom, means learning together with these people in Jesus' Way. It means not scapegoating, not being model-obstacle*s, not rivalling, not desiring, not even desiring to heal the others. It means being free at last, living together with them in abundance which is not acquired but given to us.

31. Prayer

When we pray we try to be together with God. When we pray in the name of Christ, we seek God, and to be with Him in mimesis* with Jesus, who is the image of God. When we pray, we pray to be saved from the mimesis* of desire, in mimesis* with Him outside desire, in the mimesis* which sets free.

Praying is prayer to be saved from our own ways, which are always the ways of desire, rivalry, unfreedom and unhappiness. Even the happiness of achievement is always at risk to the reverse. Praying, we ask that we might be on the Way with God, according to His will. Even when we think we know the best way for us, we still pray: Thy will, not mine.[57]

The Lord's prayer,[58] is about the Kingdom of God in every line, where He is the King of our hearts and our lives. Every sentence of it brings us on the Way of Jesus.

Our father in heaven	God is in heaven. We cannot reach Him to rival with Him. He is an external mediator.
may your name be held holy,	The name of God, His being, is 'untouchable' for us. If we touch Him, making him something like our equal, He is no longer our Father. He is a god of the scapegoaters.
your kingdom come,	He gives His kingdom, it comes to us. It is not our doing.
your will be done,	May it be given to us to do your will, doing the things we see Jesus doing, speaking the words he speaks, being outside the mimesis* of desire. In this manner we are already in the coming Kingdom.

on earth as in heaven	Let us do your will, as the angels do. They are always with you, images of you, being in mimesis* with you.
Give us today our daily bread	Let us not desire more than we need now, not even desiring that knowing that you give.
and forgive us our debts	Forgive us that time and again we go back to our old life, the life of the mimesis* of desire, so wronging each other and you.
as we have forgiven those who are in debt to us	Being together with you in prayer, we confess that it is impossible not to forgive. We no longer resent what others did to us and we confess that we did the same to them.
And do not put us to the test,	Keep us near to you, so that we will not trip up on the stumbling block and fall into the pit of desire, in whatever form it might take.
but save us from the evil one.	Save us from the devil, who is the embodiment of the mimesis* of desire, the stumbling block over which everyone who is without you falls.

Prayer is a movement, out of this culture* to God and his Kingdom. The same movement from culture* to the Kingdom is present in prayers of intercession. When we know that people are praying for us, when we know that they are going this Way for us and with us, we go the same Way in mimesis* with those who pray. This might even be true when we don't know that somebody is praying for us. We will never know what ways there are by which the hearts and lives of people meet.

32. Going the Way: The stumbling block

In the book of Acts, being in the faith* is called 'The Way'.[59] Jesus went his Way through Israel until the cross. Following him is following him on his Way. So it becomes our Way in and to freedom*. At the same time, it remains his Way.

Jesus leads us. At any time, when we don't know how to take the next step, we look to him and meet his eyes. We meet his words and actions and hope pushes us on, preventing us staying in the same spot or going backwards. The hope, which, in our relationship with Jesus, is the certainty of arrival, brings us forward.

On the Way we meet our 'skandalon', the stumbling block. Over and over, we trip up because we are too far away from Jesus and desire hits us. Although we know better, we rival. There are so many examples. We find very beautiful christian goals. We are angry with people who don't do the right things or who are wronging us or our children. We scapegoat* terrorists and scapegoaters. We act as if the other does not have the face of Jesus. For us he has the face of the devil who tries to destroy us from the beginning of the world. 'The other' can be a member of our community, our spouse, a neighbour, everybody and everything. Being on the Way we always pray: We believe, help us in our unbelieving.[60]

On this Way we are never alone, although now and again we may be without other people. Mostly, however, we are travelling together with others. We travel with people who know him as we know him. We also meet others who don't know and whom we take with us, recognising Jesus in them. We take them with us not because we wish to help them. We know that in our culture* helping is, however well-intentioned, a power-game in which the helper always stands above his or her victim, one-up in the power game. Following Jesus means being together with all men and women as we do the work and speak the words of freedom*, so hearing the words and experiencing them ourselves. We speak to and act with everybody in their own situation; politicians, dis-

turbed people, our children, ill people, fearful people, people imprisoned by their fears or imprisoned by the state, the prison or
the madhouse we put them in, and with normal people.

When we go our Way in this manner we can expect miracles.
Everybody we meet shows us the face of Christ asking us to follow him. The face may be clearly visible or deeply hidden. If we
recognise the face of Christ and we show his face to others, it
might be given to them that they recognise his face even when
they have no idea what they recognise. We know from the
gospels that every time Jesus is recognised, miracles happen. The
blind see, the deaf hear, the dead are raised and the gospel is
preached to the poor.[61] Free of the mimesis* of desire, new life begins.

When we go the Way, we give others glimpses which change
their lives as others who go the Way give us glimpses. They, like
us, might not understand what they are experiencing. Maybe
they wonder, or they experience something which they did not
expect. A person who we think we know turns out to be another
person. Lives of others change even when they do not acknowledge it.

It is not our task to erect signs of the Kingdom. If we try to do that,
we are already rivalling with reality. Our possibility is to obey
and to follow Jesus on his Way. If somebody sees, or if people see
something which changes their sense of reality, it is given to them
and to us. The Kingdom is always coming down from heaven. It
is never built up by us.

Translated into our models, Going the Way means to become a
dot. Becoming a dot is hard. It means in a sense that we die. We
can only give up our interests and desires, everything we fight
for, as though they were nothing. We come to the conclusion, as
Paul did, that we spoilt most of our lives by striving endlessly for
the good things, ultimately striving to be good.[62] Again we come
to one of the paradoxes of the gospels. By losing everything, by
opening our hands which always tried to grasp, to clasp and to
keep, they are filled with new possibilities and a new life.

33. Healing

There is no way into the new world without healing. To enter the new world means to be healed, becoming a whole, real human being, man or woman, free of inner contradictions. Healing means that we live once more in relationship with God, in non-desiring. This becomes our reality. We become free.

Healing is not the same as helping. Helping is a cultural reality – an aspect of the eternal power-game. Because it is generally accepted in culture*, helping has become a wonderful way of having power in the power-game and as such is a form of scape-goating. However well-meaning we are, this is a power-game in which the needs of others are used. The more professional our helping becomes, the more this fact becomes true. The person helped is always manipulated, played down and in the end they have to pay for it by providing the helper with a living. Of course helpers, professionals can meet in freedom*. When we see the helpless face of the other we can become a brother or sister and perhaps be enabled to give them freedom*. This is possible, al-though it is against the trend of our culture*.

Healing is a wholly other word. Indeed, healing is a very strange occurrence. Very often it simply happens. It might take place when one person meets another in his or her freedom* and in the meeting the other is healed. This story is repeated again and again in the gospels when Jesus and the disciples meet sick people.

In healing, the healer is not 'busy' with the people he meets, con-cerned about them or concerned to change them. Instead he is in freedom*, and totally with the other or others. Cultural differ-ences and the violence between them are no more. One is not more or less important than the other. If the healer does some-thing, the action arises out of his knowledge that the life of the other is blocked, the consequence of the mimesis* of desire. The causes of the illness or the difficulties lie in this mimesis*. In this situation he might do something, removing old stumbling blocks in the spatial mimesis* between him and the other. This he can do through his freedom* and the wisdom which is a part of that freedom*. Thus he can find a way to the other, a way in which both are saved.

This is true when one person meets another. It is also just as true when a single person meets a group. Groups are caught up in spatial and temporal mimesis* as well. Meeting a group in freedom* – and hence the group's powerful mimetic pressures – often means meeting those members of the group at whom all the other members are looking, the scapegoats of the group. Here too, healing is never a power game. It is always freedom* which means being without power, trusting that the Kingdom is with and for the weak.

34. The weak in our society

In comparison with Africa and Asia there are very few poor people in our society. Nobody is starving, nobody is naked. How then do we meet Christ in this world? How do we find him and as a result find ourselves? Only by meeting him can we be found by him.

In Matthew's gospel,[63] Jesus tells us that we meet him in the hungry, the thirsty, the stranger, the naked, the ill and the people in prison. They are the helpless in our society, the scapegoats of us all. In their faces, Jesus shows us his face and so ourselves.

There are still hungry and thirsty people amongst us. There are the naked, although they wear something. Certainly there are strangers, people from other races who are scapegoated immediately by us. There are also those who don't have work and can't find any, who live on the fringes of our society, driven out as the lepers once were. If they have become total outsiders, no longer seeking work and trying to make life on the fringe as livable as possible, we have made them so.

We have also done this with all the so-called mentally ill. They are people who can't live in our rivalling society, who can't live together with us. In fact we have driven them out. They are shut up in mental hospitals which are very much like prisons, often with far less freedom* than prisoners have. Now that there are too many of them and they have become inconveniently expensive for us, we throw them onto the streets where they have to linger on in their hopelessness. They are our scapegoats, as are the physically ill, who we drive out of life and shut up in hospitals where they are again used by the staff to make a living and thus they are scapegoated again. People in prison are immediately our scapegoats. Even before they are in prison, many are earmarked as future criminals and terrorists.

As a society we have an enormous scapegoating mechanism to keep our so-called normal life going. Jesus says to us: If you don't recognise me in your victims, if you don't find humanity in their helplessness, you are lost.[64] There is no healing for those we meet if we ourselves are not healed at the same time. Healing the other means recognising our own weaknesses and stopping the power-game we are in. Healing means to be converted to the weak around us, and finding our life in them. They are already God's children. Only belonging to them do we belong to God.[65]

We always speak a lot about finding ways to do this. We will certainly find them if we are prepared to go the Way, following Jesus.

35. Worship

'Think of God's mercy, my brothers, and worship him, I beg you, in a way that is worthy of thinking beings, by offering your lives and bodies as a holy sacrifice, truly pleasing to God.'[66]

Worship as a word only exists in English and means 'the veneration of power held divine' (*Oxford Dictionary of English Etymology*). Veneration means a continuing relationship, a relationship which is all-important for us and for our lives.

Knowing about Jesus and his Kingdom, the Kingdom of God, we go the Way. We are only on the Way and stay on the Way when we are together with him, in mimesis* with him. Worship means being together with God, telling each other and ourselves about his great deeds, the deeds of our salvation out of this world of the mimesis* of desire. It means speaking to and with Him, remembering Him together in the relationship with Jesus.

When we translate worship back into our models, we are in another triangle which gives space in which we can move. One point of the triangle is myself or the group of worshippers together. The second point is the world in which we are living and which in worship we can never forget. The third point is the reality of Jesus and the new world, which takes away the unclearness of this world and gives us a way through to him and the Kingdom.

In worship we remember the deeds of deliverance. We pray and speak to God. We find togetherness in Him and sing together about the great deeds – about what has happened and is happening to us.

Worship is a movement. In worship we go to the origin of our lives and our existence and thus we receive freedom* and new life. In worshipping we move through this world, following Christ with the whole of our being, together with others.

Worship requires discipline. As soon as worship does not have its own steady place, it rivals with all the other possibilities for our time, for our interests and for our hearts. When this happens, worship constantly loses out. We worship with a divided heart, hurrying to get it over with, obeying a law, not worshipping at all. We have our Sunday in order to be free of the daily havoc and rivalry, to have space to worship.

Worship needs community and perhaps needs a heart as well. We had a dream. The dream that at the place Corrymeela, whether that be in Ballycastle or elsewhere, there is a cross and near the cross day and night there are always two members praying for the community and its members, for Northern Ireland and for the world.

36. Community

When we follow Jesus and go the Way, we are never alone. We are always travelling with others. The knowledge of Christ and the following of him will never disappear.

Where two or three are gathered together in his name, where two or three know about him, he himself is there.[67] We are together with him. He offers us the possibility to follow him, to be in mimesis* with him. When we are together with him, there is always community, both with him and with each other. By being in this community, we give each other strength. We comfort each other and we show each other the Way.

This community needs shape too. Everything which does not have shape in this world is destroyed by rivalry. Of course it is true that Jesus in his reality will always break through all form and all chaos. Nevertheless, to be on the Way, and to stay on it, we need each other. We need community. We need to go on together in a manner which has shape, giving space in this world and in our lives.

The churches are such a form. Many of us belong to a church. We know that we belong together because we belong to Jesus. We also know that the boundaries between the churches and the boundaries between the churches and the rest of the world do not exist when we follow him together. Community needs form. Structure* in this case is probably too hard a word. When we are on the Way, form can change time and again.

Form also includes praying and reading together. In intercession we take each other by the hand, going together on the Way. Knowing that the others are praying for me this evening, I already go with them. My face is drawn away from the cares of this world, from all my rivalries and I look in the direction of Jesus. In praying for others I go on the Way myself.

As a community we live in the world. We are part of the world ourselves, and as a part of the world we are a community, seeking and going the Way. We take the world with us, praying for our neighbours, for our enemies, for afflicted people around us, and for those who carry great responsibilities. We trust that when we pray for them it gives them the possibility to move in greater freedom*. How this happens we don't ultimately know, and it does not matter. We know that asking God in the name of Christ, He is there and He changes things, putting feet on the Way.

From intercession stems our being together with everybody. We do what is given to us in freedom*, the expected and hopefully, more and more, the unexpected.

So we go our Way in the World taking part in the great movement in which it changes. We do it in our own manner, very often knowing nothing about 'the results'. We trust that God himself gives the fruit. We have to follow Jesus wherever he brings us, doing his works in fellowship with him.

Postscript

This enchiridion is the fruit of members of the Corrymeela Community working together. It is an attempt to reach a hand to all those who try to live on the Way, the Way of Jesus.

Many of the central themes were made clear by a Frenchman, René Girard, who has taught for many years in the USA: mimesis*, scapegoats, model-obstacle*s and so on. We are delighted with his work, which has given us and gives us so many possibilities of thinking about our place in the world and about the Ways of God and Jesus.

The face of the victim in which we recognise ourselves and rediscover our human condition, is central to the thinking of Emmanuel Levinas who was born in Lithuania and went to Western Europe after the Russian Revolution.

Much later, we met Ivan Illich and recognised ourselves in his thinking. He was born in Vienna and has lived and taught for a long time in Mexico.

It can hardly be sheer chance that those who helped us so much are all travellers. In fact we went with them, travelling.

Of course, there are many more names: Jean-Michel Oughourlian, Norbert Lofink, Raimund Schwager with many more, now hidden or in the background – though perhaps with a greater influence – who are not mentioned here. For all of them, our co-travellers, our deep thanks.

1. All terms marked * in the text are included in a short glossary of key terms on pXXX

2. Gen. 3, 1-7, esp. 6a: 'The woman saw that the tree was good to eat and pleasing to the eye, and that it was desirable for the knowledge that it could give.' Here she follows the desire of the serpent who desires that she desires. He is a stumbling block for her.

3. An example of mimesis in politics can be seen in the Falklands War. Because of its internal difficulties, Argentina needed a scapegoat, and found one in its desire of the Falklands/Malvinas. Britain had never cared about these islands, but once Argentina desired them, Britain desired them too. As a result of the desire of such an important state as Britain, Argentina desired them even more, so much so that they were prepared to sacrifice the lives of many people to get the desired object. In mimesis, British desire also grew, now also prepared to sacrifice lives to win them. In the end, Britain 'won', and took the islands. But now, because they were no longer desired, the islands were in fact useless. The desiring ended in chaos out of which the stronger emerged as 'the winner'.

In the course of hearing this story, one boy remarked that he too had discovered his Falklands. He told of how he had had a girlfriend who he had wanted to be rid of. He left her, only to find her with his friend. As soon as the friend had her, the boy wanted his former girlfriend back and did everything he could to get her. He achieved this, but once more he decided that he didn't want her. He again got rid of her and she again went out with his friend. He told that for weeks he had been plotting how to get her back. Now however, he saw what was happening and decided that his friend could keep her. Because he saw what was happening, the rivalry ended, and he saw that the girl herself was of no worth to him.

There are other examples. In the Greek tragedy, Polyneices and Eteocles, the sons of Oedipus fight with one another. In fighting, they become more and more alike. Eventually they become each other's doubles. They themselves are convinced that they are totally different from one another but onlookers cannot distinguish between them any longer. They become more and more similar. In the end they die, falling simultaneously, and in the same way, onto each others' swords. Having become exactly the same, they perish.

4. All relationships in which people are slaves of one another are like this. Many couples are enslaved to each other in this way. This eventually leads to separations which other people cannot understand because they seemed to love each other so much. Terrorists too are in model-obstacle relationships. They kill because they see it as a possibility to overcome their models, their obstacles. Even when killing, they are in deep desperation.

5. Mt 9:9: "and he said to him 'Follow me'." Following Jesus is one of the key words of the gospels.

6. Jn 5:8: 'Get up, pick up your sleeping-mat and walk.' Jesus says in fact: forget all about your rivalry with the others! I free you of it. And so he walked.

7. The gospels are very clear about this fight. cf Mt 16:25: 'For anyone who wants to save his life will lose it.'

8. Seen from this angle, the 'helping' or 'caring' professions are the professions which take care of the scapegoats of society, in the service of culture as a whole. When those working in these professions side with culture, they make sure that the scapegoats remain scapegoats in some manner or other. In a sense, culture does not wish social workers to bring the scapegoats out of their situation of distress. If the social workers side with the scapegoats, they are themselves scapegoated.

9. Ex 20:12: 'Honour your father and your mother so that you may have a long life in the land that Yahweh your God has given to you.'

10. What are the differences between the god or gods of religion and Yahweh, the father of Jesus and the God of the bible? The gods of religion are capable of every evil and good, cursing and blessing according to whim. We are totally dependent on them, though they remain as incomprehensible as the mythical scapegoat. The relationship is one of fear and subservience. These are the gods of the scapegoaters. Yahweh the father of Jesus is the god the scapegoats discovered when they were saved from the sacrifice which was intended for them by the scapegoaters. They saw (see) the world from the other side and so discovered that the gods of religion are not gods at all. Yahweh is the God without violence. He does not rival with humans as other gods do. He is omnipotent precisely through His powerlessness. Because He does not rival, He is constant in His will and actions. The relationship is one of trust. He is trustworthy. Only when we leave Him and fall into the hands of the other gods are we afraid of Him when we think of Him. But even then we are not really afraid of Him, because we don't know Him. We are afraid of the gods we are following.

11. Lk 23:34: 'Jesus said, "Father, forgive them; they do not know what they are doing."'

12. See Mk 10:18: 'Jesus said "Why do you call me good? No one is good but God alone."' The wish to be as good as he was means to wish not to be good at all.

13. Mt 23:15: 'Alas for you, scribes and pharisees, you hypocrites!'

14. Jn 8:44: 'The devil is your father and you prefer to do what your father wants.'

15. Mk 10:18: 'Jesus said to him, "Why do you call me good? No one is good but God alone."' Jesus refuses to play this game.

16. The word scapegoat appeared in Western European languages about 1600. Before that, people were not conscious of it. The appearance of the word marks the beginning of subjective hypocrisy.

17. cf. Is 43:1: 'I have called you by your name, you are mine.'

18. Lk 23:34: 'Father forgive them; they do not know what they are doing.'

19. Mt 5:45: '...for he causes his sun to rise on the bad as well as the good, and sends down rain to fall on the upright and the wicked alike.'

20. Jn 14:6-7: 'Jesus said: "I am the Way, the Truth and the Life. No one can come to the Father except through me. If you know me, you will know my father too. From this moment you know him and you have seen him."'

21. see Mt 18:20: 'where two or three meet in my name, I am there among them.' Where He is, is the new Jerusalem, the Kingdom.

22. John 13, 13: 'You call me master and Lord and rightly; because I am' (not 'and so' as in the *Jerusalem Bible*)
           likewise: John 4, 26: 'I am' not 'I am he'
                  John 6, 20: 'I am' not 'It is I'
                  John 8, 24: 'I am' not 'I am he'

23. Gen 3:6: 'The woman saw that the tree was good to eat and pleasing to the eye, and that it was desirable for the knowledge that it could give.' cf. Rom. 5,19: 'Just as by one man's disobedience many were made sinners, so by one man's obedience many will be made righteous.' Jesus, not desiring, is the new Adam. He gives a new future.

1Cor 15,45: 'the last Adam has become a life-giving spirit.'

24. To choose is a key notion in very important texts:
Deut 30:19-20: 'I set before you life or death, blessing or curse. Choose life, then, so that you and your descendants may live, in the love of Yahweh your God, obeying his voice, clinging to him.'
Josh 24–15: 'Choose today whom you wish to serve.' In the New Testament we choose by following Jesus.

25. Mk 10:29-30: 'In truth I tell you, there is no one who has left house, brothers, sisters, mother, father, children or land for my sake and for the sake of the gospel who will not be repaid a hundred times over, houses, brothers, sisters, mothers, children and land – not without persecutions-now in this present time and, in the world to come, eternal life.' cf. Matt. 11, 28-30: 'Come to me, all you who labour and are overburdened, and I will give you rest. Shoulder my yoke and learn from me, for I am gentle and humble in heart, and you will find rest for your souls. Yes, my yoke is easy and my burden light.'

26. Jn 21:19: 'After this he said, "follow me." To follow Jesus is central in the Gospels. Time and again Jesus invites us to follow him.

27. Jn 14:6: 'I am the Way, the Truth and the Life. No one can come to the Father except through me. If you know me, you know my Father too.' Also in Acts, following Christ is following the Way, for example in Acts 9, 2 where followers of Jesus are called 'followers of the Way'

28. Gen 26:22: 'He named it Rehoboth, saying, "Now Yahweh has made room for us so that we may thrive in the country."'

29. see Is 43:1-9; Is 49:1-3; Is 50:4-11; Is 52:13 - 53:12.

30. Heb 4:15: 'For it is not as if we had high priestwho was incapable of feeling our weaknesses with us, but we have one who has been tempted in every way that we are, though he is without sin.'

31. Mt 4:1-11.

32. see Jn 1.

33. Jn 8:28: 'and that I do nothing of my own accord. What I say is what the Father has taught me.' Jn 8:38: 'What I speak of is what I have seen at my father's side, and you too put into action the lessons learnt from your father.'

34. Col 1:15: 'He is the image of the unseen God.'

35. Jn 1:18: 'No one has ever seen God; it is the only Son, who is nearest to the father's heart, who has made him known.'

36. Mt 23:37: 'Jerusalem, Jerusalem, you that kill the prophets and stone those that are sent to you! How often have I longed to gather your children together, as a hen gathers her chicks under her wings, and you refused!'

37. Col 2:15: 'he has stripped the sovereignties and the powers and paraded them in public, behind him in his triumphal procession.'

38. see again Mk 10...29-30: 'In truth I tell you, there is no one who has left house, brothers, sisters, mother, father, children or land for my sake and for the sake of the gospel who will not be repaid a hundred times over, houses, brothers, sisters, mothers, children and land – not without persecutions- now in this present time and, in the world to come, eternal life.'

39. Mt 18...20: 'For where two or three meet in my name, I am there among them.'

40. Col 1:15: 'He is the image of the unseen God, the first-born of all creation.'

41. Gen 1:26: 'God said, "Let us make man in our own image in the likeness of ourselves."'

42. Mt chapters 5-7.

43. Mt 7:33-35.

44. Mt 11:25: 'I bless you , Father, Lord of heaven and of earth, for hiding these things from the learned and the clever and revealing them to little children.'

45. Jn 1:29: 'Look there is the lamb of God who takes away the sin of the world.' In fact this is saying precisely the same as Col 2:15: 'And so he has stripped the sovereignties and the powers, and paraded them in public, behind them in his triumphal procession.'

46. Lk 20:36: 'They are the same as the angels, and being children of the resurrection they are children of God.'

47. Mt 5:17: 'Do not imagine that I have come to abolish the Law or the Prophets. I have come not to abolish but to complete them.'

48. Mk 10:29-30: 'In truth I tell you, there is no one who has left house, brothers, sisters, mother, father, children or land for my sake and for the sake of the gospel who will not be repaid a hundred times over, houses, brothers, sisters, mothers, children and land – not without persecutions – now in this present time and, in the world to come, eternal life.'

49. By becoming 'helpers' of the victims of culture, our victims, we destroy them again. The only people who need help are ourselves. The only people who can help us are our victims. Again, culture is turned upside-down.

50. Acts 23:11: 'Courage! You have borne witness for me in Jerusalem, now you must do the same in Rome.'

51. see Rev 21:1-4.

52. Mt 22:30: 'For at the resurrection men and women do not marry; no they are like the angels in heaven.'

53. see Rev 21:1-14.

54. 1Cor 2:9: 'We teach what scripture calls "the things that no eye has seen and no ear has heard, things beyond the mind of man, all that God has prepared for those that love him."'

55. Heb 11:1.

56. Jn 1:29: 'Look, there is the lamb of God that takes away the sin of the world.'

57. Lk 22:42: 'Father', he said, 'if you are willing take this cup away from me. Nevertheless let your will be done not mine.' cf. Mt 6:10: 'Your will be done on earth as in heaven'

58. Mt 6:9-13.

59. Acts 9:2: 'followers of the Way' or 18, 26: Priscilla and Aquila gave 'instruction about the Way.'

60. Mk 9:24: 'I do have faith. Help my lack of faith.'

61. Lk 7:22: 'Go back and tell John what you have seen and heard: the blind see again, the lame walk, those suffering from virulent skin-diseases are cleansed, and the deaf hear, the dead are raised to life, the good news is proclaimed to the poor; and blessed is anyone who does not find a cause of stumbling in me.'

62. Phil 3:8: 'For him I have accepted the loss of everything, and look on everything as so much rubbish if only I can have Christ.' cf. Phil 2:6-7: Christ also counted his richness as nothing in order to find the other, us. As always we are here in mimesis with him.

63. Mt 25:31-46.

64. Mt 25:45: 'Then he will answer, 'In truth I tell you, in so far as you neglected to do this to one of the least of these, you neglected to do it to me.''

65. cf. Mt 5:1-10: Only by finding and giving ourselves to those who are already found by God, the blessed, can we be found ourselves.

66. Rom 12:1.

67. Mt 18:20: 'For where two or three are together in my name, I am there with them.'

A short glossary of important terms

Below are listed brief definitions of some of the key words in the text.

Culture: The possibility found by human beings to live together instead of disappearing into violence, chaos and random murder. The possibility of finding ways of keeping life in order was, and is, found by scapegoating members of the group, creating unanimity among the rest.

Faith: The existential knowledge, the knowledge of and with our very being, that we belong to the God of the scapegoats, the God of Jesus. The knowledge or knowing that He, in His powerlessness, is the only power who gives freedom, a future, a life.

Fascination: Being imprisoned in a model-rival* or a model-obstacle* relationship. When, and for as long as, the forces are balanced, or we are one-up in the relationship, it is wonderful, exciting. We call this happiness. When we are one-down, life is bleak, and eventually horrible. We are unhappy, depressed.

Freedom: Being free of the mimesis* of desire, and thus being free of all rivalry. We are free with the people around us, free of apprehensions, of anxiety and fear, having space to live and real trust for the future.

Mediation: Mimesis* 'going around' between people. Mediation* is the 'transmission' or movement of mimesis* from one to the other and back. In fact mimesis* is going around simultaneously in many different ways in the lives of everybody.
> *External Mediation*: There are differences between the model and the other. We have our own places. There is transcendence* which we obey. Model-model* relationships are relationships in which there is no rivalry, in which teaching and
> learning are possible.
> *Internal Mediation*: The mediation* between us is direct. There are no boundaries between us, no structures. Transcendence* has disappeared. We fall victim to one

another immediately in model-rival* and model-obstacle* relationships.

Mimesis: I am feeling, thinking, doing as you are without knowing that I am imitating you, without being conscious of it. Mimesis* always happens before we think. It is not imitation. Mimesis* is the condition of our human life together. We are always in mimesis*, for the whole of our lives.

Mimesis of Desire: As human beings, we are always desiring something: Food, clothes, a man, a woman, a car, a position, fame or whatever. Being in mimesis* with one another we are all always desiring and, as a result, we are always liable to rival with one another if there is no external mediation*.

Metaphysical Desire: Ultimately, our deepest desire is not just for things but the desire to be. We desire being. In the mimesis* of desire, we don't trust. We desire, wishing that we can cope without trusting others, that we can simply 'be'. Ultimately, we try to take the being of somebody else for ourselves, somebody more important in our eyes than we are. Through their being we seek being for ourselves.

Temporal Mimesis: As children, we learn everything: We learn to do things, we learn to be human. We learn by being in mimesis* with our mother, our father, other people around us. We learn by repeating time and again what we have learned, by doing again what we have already done. This is a big part of our life, temporal mimesis*. Indeed this is our normal life. In fact, in this manner we even repeat things our ancestors did without knowing it.

Spatial Mimesis: All of our life we are in spatial mimesis*. spatial mimesis* is the mimesis* that is happening in the space where we are at any moment with the people and human realities around us. The possibilities for change in our lives, whether for better or of or worse, are in spatial mimesis*.

Models: Our model is the person, the group, the human reality with which we are in mimesis*. We are never immediately conscious of it. Mostly, we are never conscious of it.

Model-model: We are in model-model* relationships when we are not in rivalry with our model. a model has his or her place and we have our own places as well. We respect each other and each other's places. Model-model* relationships are relationships in which learning can really take place. It is the place of (cultural) freedom*.

Model-rival: A model-rival* is a person or a human reality with whom or which we rival, trying to have what the other has. In the end we are only trying to win in the rivalry. Ultimately it is a rivalry for being. When or if we win in the rivalry, we discover that our desires are not fulfilled, that, in fact, we won nothing. we begin to rival again. Rivalrous life is exciting for as long as we are not constant losers. However, if we end up as constant losers we become depressed, and might even find ourselves in model-obstacle* relationships.

Model-obstacle: A model-obstacle* is a model over whom, or which, we can certainly never win. In these relationships we are obsessed by winning over somebody or something very big or important. Our dream is that by winning over this other person, we can become even more important than they are. This is why, without knowing it, we seek invincible models. Of course, if it ever appears that we might actually win, we make the model even more important, even bigger, even higher. The fact that we might win would show that the rivalry was actually about nothing — that it was not worth trying. Being in a model-obstacle* relationship means that we are totally imprisoned by the relationship. We are extremely elated and extremely unhappy alternately. In the end we are totally depressed, even having thoughts of suicide.

Religion: Religion* is the result of the scapegoat* mechanism. The killed scapegoat* is a god and a devil. Religion* adores this god who is, at the same time, the devil-god. Religion is never being sure if he is a god and therefore good or the devil and therefore bad. To religion* belong myths, stories about the driving out of the scapegoat*, rites, repetitions of the driving out, and prohibitions. Although through secularisation, religion* is sinking further away from our consciousness and out of reach for us, our whole culture* and life are still built on religion*. In a deep sense, religion* and culture* are one.

Scapegoat: The scapegoat* is the random victim of a group in deep trouble. A group in serious trouble (cf. a saloon-bar scene in a Western), cannot, and does not, find rational possibilities to solve its problems. A random member of the group is chosen to be the culprit and s/he is smitten, driven out. After the ejection, there is peace again. For the people who did the driving out, this means that s/he was obviously the cause of all the trouble, the devil, because there is peace again. At the same time, s/he must have something to do with peace. S/he gave it to us, because after s/he is driven out, the peace returns. Thus s/he is a god. In this manner, the conditions for culture* to come into existence were met. We still use the scapegoat* to be able to get along with each other and to get rid of our own responsibility.

Structure: Structure* is the order in culture*, in society, which developed through a very long process in order to keep peace in society. Peace is only possible when people are different, each having their own place, which is respected by everybody. In structure*, model-model* relationships are possible. When structure* disappears, as it is doing now, all relationships become model-rival* and model-obstacle* relationships. Everybody becomes unfree.

Transcendence: Transcendence* is a reality 'above' us, out of our reach, which gives shape and meaning to our lives. It might be the god of the scapegoaters, of religion. It might be duty or respect for human beings. The God of the scapegoats, who is powerless, who showed himself in Jesus and shows himself in every person who is suffering, turns transcendence around. Everything is turned around in the gospel. God is no longer 'above' us, as in religion, but around and beneath us. In the sense of religion and culture, this God is powerless.